The Taoist Alchemy
of Wang Liping

The Taoist Alchemy
of Wang Liping

Volume 1

By Nathan Brine

Foreword by Wang Liping

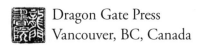 Dragon Gate Press
Vancouver, BC, Canada

The information in this book is not intended to replace the guidance of a qualified teacher, nor advice from a medical practitioner and should be used solely at the reader's discretion. The author and publisher disclaim any liability or loss, personal or other, resulting from the information in this book.

Cover Image: relief carving detailing the traditional Chinese story of the fish that turned into a dragon by jumping over the Dragon Gate.

Editing: Daniel Mahlberg and Derek Gladwin
Design: Sanghi Choi

Contents

PART TWO: THEORY

PART THREE: SUPPLEMENTAL PRACTICES

PART FIVE: ENTERING THE GATE, CONTINUED

Chapter 16: Training with Wang Liping, Part Two 169

Epilogue 181

APPENDICES

Appendix 1: Overview of the Dragon Gate System 185

Appendix 2: Glossary... 191

Foreword

Hello friends!

My name is Wang Liping. I was born in China in 1949. In my early youth, I was initiated into the Taoist Complete Reality Dragon Gate Lineage as the 18th-Generation successor and transmitter. The masters who initiated me were 16th-Generation Zhang Hedao (*shiye*), 17th-Generation Wang Jiaoming (*shifu*), and 17th-Generation Jia Jiaoyi (*shifu*). I was given the Taoist name: Eternal Life (*Yongsheng*). The Taoist Complete Reality Dragon Gate Lineage specializes in cultivating the secret methods of the Golden Elixir (internal alchemy or *neidan*) and the Taoist Five Arts: fate calculation, appearance discernment, divination, practices, and medicine. I was chosen by my masters to be the official successor and transmitter of the Dragon Gate Lineage.

Nathan Brine is my good friend! Nathan has cultivated and practiced internal alchemy for many years gaining a deep understanding of its profound mystery. And now, through teaching, Nathan has been able to increase his comprehension and embodied experience of Taoist alchemy even more. Chinese Taoism takes "the Way (dao) models itself on what is naturally so" as foundation, takes the changes of *yin* and *yang* as the means, and takes the uniting of stillness and movement as the way to practice. Taoist practice allows the practitioner to transcend the ordinary and enter the realm of the immortals, to live a long and healthy life, and become one with all that is.

Several years ago, during a conversation with Nathan in Singapore, the idea of writing a book about the practice came up. Nathan thought it would be a good idea to publish a book based on his own experience practicing and teaching Taoist alchemy. This book would help more people know about the Chinese Taoist practice of internal alchemy, allowing more people to heal, become healthy and live a long life. After years of hard work, my good friend Nathan has completed Volume 1 of this series explaining the secret methods of the golden elixir. Congratulations Nathan Brine!

Most people figure that Taoist alchemy is some form of incomprehensible metaphysics that is either too hard to understand or simply unbelievable. Actually, it is a crystallization of Chinese wisdom. Taoist alchemy teaches us how to use our own spirit to understand ourselves. The secret methods of the Golden Elixir teach us how to change our body and mind, and to use our body and mind to heal and find our own light. Our existence is temporary, and the future is far away. Not only do we need light, but as practitioners we can also share our inner and outer light with the world, allowing the people of the world to share in health, happiness and good fortune!

I hope this book can help practitioners find a little light of the Tao!

June 9th, 2019 Dalian
Wang Liping

各位朋友道友大家！

我是中国王力平，49年生人，少年拜道教全真龙门派十六代张合道为师爷，拜道教全真龙门派十七代王教明、贾教义为师父，传承道教全真龙门派第十八代 我王力平—永生。专修"金丹秘法"及道家"五术"：命、相、卜、山、医之道法。我是师爷、师父认定的、道教全真龙门派本门支脉第十八代继承人、传代人。

道明是我好友！修炼金丹秘法多年，深得其中奥秘，在教授学生中有更多的感悟和体验。中国道家以道法自然为理念基础、以阴阳变化为手段，以动静结合为修炼方法。使修炼者能达到超凡入仙，长生久视，天人合一境界。

几年前在新加坡与道明交谈中，他想写一本自已修炼与教学金丹秘法一些感悟分享给更多的朋友，让更多的人知道有一种中国道家修炼方法金丹秘法，可使人少疾无病，健康长寿！经几年的努力，好友道明、金丹秘法感悟第一稿的完成，恭喜道明！

大多数人认为金丹秘法是不可思议的，形而上学的玄学，其实它是中国人智慧的结晶，是用自己的心灵来了解自己的一种方法。用金丹秘法的修炼方法，改变自己的身心，使身心得到健康而光明！我们的存在是暂时的，未来是遥远的，不仅我们自己需要光明，而且修炼者可以把自身内外的光明分享给世界，从而让世界众生共同康宁、快乐、幸福！

希望借此书，给修炼爱好者引来一点道光之明！

王力平
2019年6月9日于大连

Acknowledgments

First and foremost, I wish to thank my teacher, Wang Liping. Thank you for opening the Dragon Gate. Without you I could never have realized the depth and profundity of Taoist practice. Without your constant encouragement and advice, I would not have started teaching, nor would I have written this book. I am deeply grateful for the incredible hard work and sacrifices you have made in passing the Dragon Gate Lineage on to us. Thank you so much!

This book could not have been written without the understanding and support of my wife. Thank you for believing in me, Michelle! Thank you for supporting me through all the years of hard training. As practitioners, it is difficult to succeed without our families behind us. Thank you so much, Baby!

Thank you Shamira Rahim for keeping me aligned in more ways than one, and being the life coach I needed. You believed in me before I did. Thank you!

Thanks to my book team for helping make this project happen. Thanks to Daniel Mahlberg and Derek Gladwin for your superlative editing chops, and to Sanghi Choi for your beautiful design sense. Thanks, team, for your dedication and hard work in making this project a reality!

Along the way, I have been blessed with many great teachers. Thank you Marvin Lampert and Paul Crowe for setting me on the path in the right direction, and thank you to all the teachers who keep me going: Feng Zhiqiang, Chen Yu, Gu Mingwei, Nelson Ma, Zhang Jingfa, Losang, Li Rong, and Dr. Zhuo Tongnian.

I also want to thank my students. I have the best job in the world. The only thing I love more than practicing Taoist cultivation is sharing it. You are all amazing people!

Finally, thanks to all my friends for your help and support. The Taoist classics say that finding a Taoist friend to share the way with is even harder than finding a Taoist teacher. Fortunately, this has not been true for me. Thanks to all my training partners over the years, such as Matthew Huggett, Marin Spivak, Tom Evdokimoff, and Joshua Lenti-Jones, just to name a few. And last but not least, the Banlü Crew: Scotty Ellis, Catalina Alexandra, Mark Bartosh, Manish Bhatt, and Sandra Podhajsky.

Introduction

In China's Henan province, along the middle reaches of the Yellow River, lie a series of rapids known as the Dragon Gate. The water holds many fish, some that swim upstream against the formidable current. According to Chinese legend, any fish that manages to leap the Dragon Gate's final waterfall is rewarded for its perseverance through transformation into the most esteemed of beings—an immortal dragon. This story of triumph in the face of adversity lends its name to the Taoist Dragon Gate Lineage or *Longmen pai* and its practice of internal alchemy, also referred to as *neidan*. Internal alchemy, the "Way of the Golden Elixir," is a system of transformation. Like the fish who endeavours to turn into a dragon, the Taoist alchemist seeks to change the self through a process of energetic refinement.

Internal alchemy (*neidan*) is complex and multilayered. Seeking to transform the self, the practitioner sits cross-legged, enters a meditative state, follows guided instructions, and achieves specific results through the careful coordination of body, breath, and awareness. Some describe this process as practicing qigong while meditating. Qigong, or energy practice, is the modern Chinese term for working with energy, and *neidan* fits under the same rubric. However, Taoist alchemy goes much deeper. *Neidan* not only seeks to tune into and build up energy, but also to transform it into a purer, more rarified state.

Wang Liping, whose story will be chronicled in the next chapter, is the teacher responsible for transmitting the Dragon Gate Lineage to the next generation. Over the years, he has shared a diverse range of techniques. While it can be fun and informative to try out a variety of practices, excess content can prove not only distracting but even intimidating, especially for a new student.

For this reason, I will outline in the following chapters a core curriculum to keep our practice on track. Over the course of 10 chapters, I present the skills needed to create an energetic sphere inside our body called an Elixir. While there are several different kinds of elixirs, the one defined in this book is called the Lesser

Reverted Elixir. This Elixir is formed by refining energy associated with our physical body called *jing* into a more rarified form called *qi*. To form this Elixir, we will work on the internal organs of the body and opening the Maoyou Cosmic Orbit.

Discussions of elixirs and energy centres can become a little abstract, so I will also share my own experiences with *neidan*, seeking to anchor alchemical methods and techniques with descriptions from my own practice. The book begins and ends with the details of my first three years training with Wang Liping.

One of the reasons I decided to write this book is because English-language *neidan* resources continue to be rare. Many of the famous Dragon Gate Lineage practices remain largely unknown to English speakers. This book is an attempt to begin rectifying this situation and make more resources available to non-Chinese-language practitioners. However, translating Taoist Classical Chinese is notoriously difficult. When translating a text, a choice is often necessarily made between clarity and meaning. Although I wrote this book from the ground up in English to maintain clarity, Chinese and Taoist terms have been used throughout in an effort to keep the instructions grounded in their original tradition. You may wish to familiarize yourself with some of the core Chinese terms mentioned in the glossary.

There is no need to read the book cover to cover. The book opens with a short description of Dragon Gate Taoism and Wang Liping. Chapter 2 begins a detailed account of my training with Wang Liping, which is concluded in Chapter 16. Theory helpful for *neidan* practice will be addressed in Chapter 3. In Chapter 4, Foundation, I discuss the importance of preparing the body and mind for *neidan* practice. However, the best way to learn about Taoist practice is simply to experience it firsthand by doing it. Feel free to start with Chapter 5, Stillness. The core techniques that follow the stillness chapter are meant to be followed sequentially. Chapters 12 to 15 present some of the supplemental practices. The final chapter concludes my first three years training with Wang Liping. A glossary of alchemy terms and an overview of Wang Liping's Dragon Gate system finishes the book.

Finally, *neidan* is an advanced practice, and there are limits to what you will be able to achieve without an instructor. This book is meant as an introduction and resource for students. However, gaining any real traction with the methods in this book will require personal instruction. Given proper guidance and sufficient effort, however, the potential rewards are profound. I hope you find this book a helpful resource on your journey.

PART ONE

Entering the Gate

1.

Wang Liping and Dragon Gate Taoism

Taoism

When I first started practicing Taoist practice, I did not really understand it. Normally, I felt comfortable around esoteric Asian spirituality. My mother was a meditation, tai chi, and qigong practitioner, and my father had a Tibetan Buddhist teacher. I also had a passing familiarity with some South Asian religions, which basically meant I had read a book or two on the subject. Nevertheless, Taoism always remained a little removed. Even its name was unclear to me: Taoism or Daoism? I was not alone. According to modern scholars, Taoism remains the least understood of the world's major spiritual traditions.

In the Chinese language, Taoism literally means Teachings of the Way (*daojiao* 道教). Returning to the Way, or *dao*, means to return to the source of our being. In ancient times, *dao* was synonymous with *qi* 氣, or energy. This brings us to the main conceptual shift needed to understand Taoism: it's all about *qi*. However, *qi* is not something we think about. Along with the *dao*, *qi* is something we experience.

For some, Taoism is a religion; for others, it is a philosophy. But neither of these two Western terms do much justice to the richness and vastness of the Taoist experience. Even the term Taoism is problematic, suggesting a unified school or way of thinking. When I was studying Taoist studies in university and graduate school, the main issue scholars wrestled with was the very definition of Taoism itself. But this is not necessarily a bad thing. It speaks to the heart of Taoism. The Taoist experience lies outside of the conceptual mind and the need for categorization. It is not something we think about, it is something we practice, experience, and embody.

There are many kinds of Taoism. The tradition has been around in one form or another for a least 2,500 years, and throughout this long history, there have been many manifestations of Taoist practice. This deeply embedded cultural perspective has influenced many aspects of traditional Chinese life. Chinese martial arts, mysticism, medicine, philosophy, politics, and religion have all been shaped by the Taoist experience. At various times, Taoism was also expressed, in various phases, as what westerners would identify as institutionalized religion—or a formalized study on a mass, collective scale. Distilling Taoism into to one concrete definition, however, is perhaps not very useful.

The easiest way to make sense of Taoism is through lineages (*liupai* 流派), which are lines of transmission that can be found throughout Chinese culture. In historical China, if someone wanted to learn something, they would find a teacher. Skills such as learning to cook, repairing shoes, painting a picture, and building a bridge were all passed on from teacher to apprentice. Often these teachers would have a lineage, a line developing from the teacher, to the teacher's teacher, and so on. The lineage encapsulated the combined experience and knowledge of previous teachers. The line also identified both the teacher and the transmitted skill. It not only situated the teacher within the vast social network of relationships that is so important to Chinese society, but it also embedded the student within a vast mosaic of personal connections.

Taoism is no different. Taoism is an artisanal practice passed on through lineages, each with its own collection of knowledge and practices. The essence and practice of Taoism varies depending on the nature of each lineage. A relationship to a teacher and their teachings is of greater significance than the label of Taoist. In appreciating the role of lineage, a clearer picture of Taoism appears.

Dragon Gate Lineage

In this book, I share the Dragon Gate Lineage (*Longmen pai* 龍門派) transmitted by Wang Liping 王力平 and founded by the 13th-century master Qiu Chuji 丘處機 with the help of his teacher (Wang Chongyang 王重陽) and his teacher's teachers (Lü Dongbin 呂洞賓 and Zhongli Quan 鍾離權). Dragon Gate is primarily known for its practice of internal alchemy or *neidan* 內丹.

Wang Liping

Wang Liping is the 18th heir, holder, and transmitter of the Dragon Gate Lineage of Complete Reality Taoist practice. His traditional mountain lineage (*shandao* 山道) is concerned primarily with practice and self-transformation. Although mountain lineages have some interaction with temple lineages (*jiadao* 家道), they are not bound to any institution other than the lineage.[1] Wang Liping was

---

1   There are three main kinds of Taoist lineage: mountain, temple, and domestic. Bear in mind, the distinction between these lineages is often blurred. Their interaction is complex and changes depending on location and historical period.

confirmed by three masters of the lineage, and his arduous training has been documented in Thomas Cleary's translated book *Opening the Dragon Gate: The Making of a Modern Taoist Wizard.*

I like to think of Wang Liping as a vessel carrying the Dragon Gate teachings to the next generation. The modernization of China over the last several decades had a turbulent effect on traditional culture, Taoism included. Many cultural artifacts were lost, while powerful lineages were erased. My sense is that Wang Liping's teachers knew the storm was coming and chose Wang Liping as their insurance plan. Over the course of 15 years, they loaded as much as possible into their young apprentice. Wang Liping became solely responsible not only for mastering the training material, but also for transmitting it to subsequent generations. It was a heavy charge.

Wang Liping was born in 1949 in Northeast China. The three masters first selected and then began training him when he was 12 years old. Over the next 15 years, Wang Liping "ate bitter"—a Chinese term for working hard toward a goal where you need to eat bitter to taste sweet. For the first few years of his training, Wang Liping lived with his family. He would meet the three old Taoists daily after school in an abandoned warehouse on the outskirts of the city. During these visits, Wang Liping's teachers introduced him to the various practices of the lineage: *neidan*, the core of the teaching, and the Five Taoist Arts of fate calculation, appearance discernment (includes physiognomy and feng shui), divination, practice (includes ritual and martial arts) and medicine. Under the guidance of his three masters, Wang Liping began his practice.

During the Cultural Revolution (c. 1966–1976), Wang Liping and his three teachers hit the road. Travel for spiritual development is an important part of Taoist practice. Called Cloud Wandering (*yunyou* 雲遊), this mode of travel is a type of pilgrimage involving training and the exchange of information with other Taoists. Wang Liping and his teachers spent years on the road, sticking to backroads and mountain villages while seeking out sacred sites and other places of Taoist significance. Wang Liping speaks warmly of these early years. It is clear that, to this day, he still misses his teachers and the time they spent together.

In the late 1970s, Wang Liping went to Tibet to learn directly from the Panchen Lama, immersing himself in the study of Tibetan esoteric tantric practice. In Taoist practice, after initiates reach a certain level of accomplishment, their teachers often encourage them to seek out other masters. Tibetan Buddhism and Taoism shared a close relationship over the centuries. After Wang Liping's time in Tibet, he returned to the normal world, got married, found a job, and began his new life and training as a domestic Taoist, incorporating his Taoist training with everyday responsibilities.

At this time, qigong 氣功 was starting to gain popularity in China. Energy practice has been a central fixture of the Chinese cultural landscape for thousands of years. It underpins everything from medicine to the art of sexual relationships. In the 1950s, the Chinese government drew on this wealth of knowledge to promote the healthy practices for the Chinese people. Qigong became a cheap and effective healthcare alternative. As qigong gained momentum in the 1980s, some people started looking beyond the superficial health benefits to the roots of the practice. One obvious source was Taoist alchemy, and who could be better situated to teach than Wang Liping, the official transmitter of the Dragon Gate Lineage?

Wang Liping started teaching publicly in 1985. He stepped back from public teaching in 1995 and resumed in 2005 to address an international audience. Since then he has taught continually both in China and around the world.

Taoist Identity

In the West, it is customary to identify with our religious faith: I am Christian, I am Muslim, I am Jewish. In China, however, spiritual identity is more fluid and socially bound. In the old days, a Taoist practitioner would not call themselves a Taoist unless it was their job or vocation. An adherent working in the temple would be considered a Taoist, but a layman spending time at the temple would not. Religious exclusivity never gained much traction in China. Contrary to the West, where it is common to consider oneself a Christian and only a Christian, in China you can freely and simultaneously participate in different kinds of spirituality, for each avenue is perceived as having something unique and valuable to offer.

2.

Training with Wang Liping, Part One

During our discussions about writing this book, Wang Liping and I agreed that explaining my own experiences as a practitioner offers the best path to begin. At first, I was hesitant. Over time, however, I realized that sharing my own experiences would make Taoist alchemy more accessible to readers. Taoist insight is not a theoretical pursuit; it is achieved by the experience gained through practice. It changes us, and in so doing, it deepens our understanding of ourselves and the world around us. These changes prove the merit of the practice. Experience takes priority over theory in Taoism.

Wang Liping encourages his students to keep a practice journal. Besides its many intrapersonal benefits, journaling facilitates the gift of research and self-exploration. There is precious little info available about practitioners' experiences along the road of Taoist internal alchemy (*neidan*). Data on the broader project of cultivation preserves a record for those interested in the results of Taoist practice; the more we have, the clearer this project becomes.

In this chapter, I draw from my journal to detail my initial meeting with Wang Liping, my early training experiences, and the changes I have undergone since immersing myself in the world of Taoist alchemy. I have selected personal experiences from the first three years of my training, during which time my story is to some degree analogous with the practices detailed later in this book. The first half is included here. The second half can be found at the end of the book in Chapter 16. By bookending the practices with my personal experiences, I hope to inform and inspire the reader to the possibilities of Taoist practice. If biography is not your bag, feel free to skip over this chapter.

Beginning

I did not know what to expect when I signed up for my first retreat with Wang Liping. I had been looking for a *neidan* teacher for 15 years. The challenge of this search made me more and more cynical. Very little information was available about Wang Liping or what he actually taught. After several years of searching in China, and several more years researching Taoist practices in university, I had come to think that authentic Taoist alchemy had disappeared along with so many other cultural treasures of yesteryear. The Chinese have a term for it: *shi chuan* 失傳 or lost transmission.

Years before, I had read a book about Wang Liping entitled *Opening the Dragon Gate: the Making of a Modern Taoist Wizard*. Although the book detailed his early training, it was hard to know how much of it was folktale or truth. I had no context for it. I still had so much to experience with my own training before I could begin to make sense of it. The literary style of the story did not help; it was written in the shadow of a Chinese literary tradition that wrapped Taoist practice in a cloak of mystery and legend. The interspersed scientific discussions were unconvincing. The sensationalized and idealized accounts of Wang Liping's training did not help. The depth of the book was lost on me. But I am getting ahead of myself.

It all started in the spring of 1997, when I began my Taoist practice. Tai chi (*taiji quan* 太極拳) was my way in. I had been curious about tai chi for a year or perhaps longer, but I was hesitant to commit. I remember asking my mother, who had practiced for several years, "So what is this tai chi stuff about anyway. Is it just slowly waving your hands around in the air? Boring!" My 20-year-old self could not make sense of it.

One day, as I was riding the city bus through downtown Vancouver, a sign for a tai chi school appeared with the Taoist *yin* and *yang* symbol emblazoned on the side of the building. A rush of tingles went up my spine. I quickly got off the bus and went inside to sign up.

Tai chi is a martial art often used for health, and is not, in and of itself, Taoist practice. But somehow, quite coincidentally, my first two teachers were Taoists. Marvin Lampert and Paul Crowe were initiates within a Taoist lineage from Guangzhou via Hong Kong. They introduced me to internal practice (*neigong* 內功), meditation (*jingzuo* 靜坐), and the Taoist temple arts of chanting, ceremonies, and altar care. My first teachers also taught me a rare internal martial art called *liuhebafa* 六合八法 or "water boxing", which I practiced under their guidance for three years.

Most importantly, they exposed me to the Taoist mode of cultivation, something that is hard to learn from a book. As Paul Crowe put it, one learns Taoism through a kind of cultural osmosis. This Taoist perspective became my lodestone: it directed from who I learned and what I trained. It still does today.

Within Taoist circles, it is considered bad form to explicate the Taoist perspective. For now, I will just say that Taoists tend to privilege experience over intellect.

In other words, do not think, practice—or at least let practice lead the thoughts. Accordingly, I put my practice first and began building my foundation.

I worked as a part-time restaurant server in order to pay the bills. I used the rest of my time to practice. I was hungry to learn anything related to the Chinese internal arts. *Liuhebafa* and tai chi remained my core practice. They seemed an ideal vehicle to build the Taoist body. During this period, I also studied qigong, *neigong*, meditation, various kinds of martial arts, and Taoist temple arts. I spent a year practicing with a Buddhist Shaolin qigong teacher and healer from Shanghai, named Zhang Jinfa 張金發. I tried a little modern martial arts (*wushu* 武術) and qigong with a Szechuanese lady named Li Rong. I enrolled in Mandarin classes. I even did a stint apprenticing with a doctor of classical Chinese medicine, Dr. Zhuo Tongnian 卓同年. It was all fun. I loved it.

During my first year of practice, I stumbled on a book about Taoist internal alchemy. It immediately hooked me in and I wanted to learn as much as possible. One core principle these experiences taught me was that I could not learn these methods from a book. I needed a teacher. Subsequently, I checked everywhere for a teacher and asked everyone I knew in the internal arts world. My current Taoist teachers told me that if I wanted to engage in high-level Taoist practice like alchemy, I first needed a foundation. So, that is what I did. I kept working on my foundation.

In retrospect, I realize now that in those days I never really excelled at what I was practicing. What I did learn was how to focus and how to train, as well as how to improve my health and basic body conditioning. I also discovered *qi*. The first time I distinctly felt my *qi* was after I started practicing standing meditation. I had done standing postures before but not consistently. Then I decided to stand every day, and that is when things really started to change. On day five, I had rushes of shivers shoot up my back to the top of the head. It felt amazing. After the session, all I could do was sit down and literally look up and watch the clouds go by. I was in some sort of heightened state of bliss. At work that night, I continued to have rushes of *qi* throughout my body. That is when I really got the importance of daily practice.

China

After five years of practice, I began yearning for more. I wanted to immerse myself completely in my training and find its source. China was calling, so off I went to explore. My first stop was Anhui province, where one of my teachers was opening a martial arts and qigong school. The school did not work out—the year was 2001 and qigong in China was not doing very well—but there was no way I was going back to Vancouver. I loved life in China. And I still had my mission: to train and develop *gong* 功, the acquired development of embodied skill. The Chinese view the concept of *skill* as not just a mental capability but something that is built into the body through hard work over years of practice. I wanted it—I wanted *gong*.

My next stop was Beijing. I had a friend there who helped me to secure an introduction to the Chen family tai chi and qigong teacher, Feng Zhiqiang 馮志強. I had been practicing Chen's tai chi for a few years already and Feng Zhiqiang seemed like the right fit. For one thing, he was from a traditional lineage. By this point, I had learned that there was a line of demarcation within the Chinese martial arts world: traditional vs. modern.

Traditional practices are passed from teacher to student through lineages; modern practices are watered down versions endorsed by state-sanctioned institutions. The goal of traditional martial arts is to learn the principles of the art; sets of movements are simply a means of expressing and developing those principles. With traditional tai chi, you start with movement, but then you practice and refine those movements over years, learning the internal principles and the martial applications. The movements continually evolve as you evolve. Learning is endless.

With modern tai chi, you learn a simplified shell of the movements, practice it intensely for a few months until it looks good, then move on to a new form. It can be a useful vehicle for developing physical conditioning, but it misses the depth of the art. I had experience with both types of practice, and for me there was no comparison: traditional was my path. So, in the spring of 2002, I started training at Feng Zhiqiang's school.

I practiced full time. I found a cheap apartment in the university district of Beijing and took the subway to class every morning. Class lasted four hours long, seven days a week. I practiced at night for another hour or so on my own. Life was good. We did tai chi and qigong, with lots of standing practice (*zhanzhuang* 站椿). Feng Zhiqiang was incredible. To this day, some of the best kung fu (*gongfu* 功夫) I have seen or felt came from him. His *qi* was massive. His movements were incredibly soft. But it was his stillness that impressed me the most. When he practiced, it was as if all the sounds of the city disappeared. He radiated stillness.

The practice was beneficial and engaging but I started to get bored. My body started to change. Although my teacher was amazing, I kept getting the sense that something was missing in the training. Feng Zhiqiang did not teach much content at this point; he had just taken his final disciple, closing the door to the inner training.

Chinese culture is complicated. If you want to learn an art, it is not enough to just go and find a teacher. Traditional teachers keep certain things for certain students. Think of Google's search engine algorithm. It is secret. Even if you go to Google and request to see it, you probably would not get the chance. Google needs to trust you and have a reason to reveal it. The same applies to learning traditional Chinese arts.

In Chinese culture, there is public and private. The metaphor for this is a door: moving past the door means becoming part of the family and receiving the private good stuff. And there is good stuff. My lack of Chinese language skills was the main problem. My Chinese language skills needed significant improvement, even though I knew enough to learn the practice. Regardless, I needed better Chinese to get through the door, and through the door is exactly where you want to be.

Then I met my next teacher. One day in September 2002, my American friend, Marin Spivak, gave me a call. "I found him. I found the man. This is the guy I've been searching for these past three years." He was talking about Chen family tai chi teacher Chen Yu 陳瑜, the only son of Chen Zhaokui 陈照奎 and the grandson of legendary Chen practitioner Chen Fake 陳發科. I mean, talk about the source of Chen family tai chi: this guy grew up in and inherited Chen Fake's house. Marin had been searching the parks of Beijing for a few years already, trying to find a lead. Marin knew Chen Yu existed and he knew he was good. But where was he—and did he even teach?

Back then, the internet was still in its infancy, and there were no phone directories in China. When Marin finally found him, he asked if I wanted to tag along? Well, I thought, why not? So, I began three years of some of the most intensive training up until this point.

Chen Yu was good, really good. I had never seen Chen family tai chi like this; even now, with all the video footage bouncing around on YouTube, I have not seen anything like it. The real stuff was never videotaped, let alone shown in public. You had to be there on the right day with the right students before he unleashed it. The moves were all spine and spirals. I am sure Feng Zhiqiang knew some of this, but Chen Yu was young and ready to make his mark on the world. This is, I think, largely why he decided to teach it.

They say with all good teachers, there are windows of opportunity. Too young and their skills are not fully developed; too old and their disciples take on most of the teaching. With Chen Yu, that window was the first decade of the new millennia. We trained seven days a week. No matter how dire the weather, we were there with Chen Yu. We ate bitter and the training was nasty. The stance and body method (*shenfa* 身法) were brutal to practice. But every class felt like the veil being lifted. Chen Yu made the inner mechanics of each move obvious, showing how the spine drives everything to produce a specific force (*jin* 勁). I enjoyed life. I drank *baijiu*.[1] I had fun. I was even initiated into the Chen family lineage as a 20th generation disciple of Chen Yu.

---

1 *Baijiu* is a potent kind of wine often imbibed in Northern China.

The question kept coming back to me: where was the Taoist stuff? I received a taste of it from my first teachers and wanted more. Throughout my time in Beijing, I kept my mission clear and built my foundation. I used tai chi as a vehicle to develop my body and mind for *neidan*. Nothing had yet to materialize. Finding a teacher of Taoist self-cultivation, let alone *neidan*, is no easy task.

As I had learned from tai chi, skill varied greatly between teachers. I had come across one or two Taoists during my time in Beijing, but they mostly stayed private and refrained from teaching. So, I decided to try my luck in Taiwan.

I arrived in Taiwan in 2005. Traditional Chinese culture had fared better in Taiwan, and I hoped to find what I was looking for there. Although I continued to explore the internal martial arts scene, attending a number of tai chi and bagua classes, I began to prioritize daily sitting meditation over the tai chi I had learnt from Chen Yu. I also started meeting with a Tibetan Buddhist monk who was teaching meditation and giving talks on the Dharma. It was a welcomed change of pace from the Kungfu world. I enjoyed my time in Taiwan, but my search for a Taoist teacher was unsuccessful. After several years of living in the Far East, the visa I needed to live there did not come through. I was forced to return to Canada. This ending became fortuitous for a new beginning, the journey I had been searching for many years.

Back to Canada

As I had planned on living the rest of my life in Asia, returning to Vancouver was a shock. I was 29 years old and the only real skill I had was Mandarin; even my tai chi had not developed to a level where I felt comfortable teaching. I decided to enroll at the University of British Columbia, which just happens to have one of the largest Asian Studies departments in the world. I stayed for eight years, completing an honours degree in Asian Language and Culture and then, in graduate school, exploring the intersection of *neidan* and tai chi in the late Qing Dynasty. I worked on Classical Chinese language, history, philosophy, religion, literature, and as much Taoist material as I could devour. I enjoyed life. I drank coffee. I had fun.

During this period, I also stumbled onto a Wu family tai chi teacher, Gu Mingwei 顧明偉. I began practicing with Gu Mingwei shortly after my return. I honestly cannot remember why I switched from Chen to Wu tai chi. I remember needing a place to work out and had heard good things about Wu family tai chi in general, especially their push hand (*tuishou* 推手) and application (*sanshou* 散手) skills. Gu Mingwei did not disappoint. I practiced with him for 10 years. His art is deep and subtle but effective. His skill is not obvious until you touch hands with him. Traditional Wu family tai chi is alive in Vancouver, and while I love knowing that it will be passed on, I could not for the life of me become proficient. It is that hard.

The difficulty with Wu's tai chi is the need to "sink" instantly before any technique is applied (see boxed text on page 37: *Song and Sinking*). My body was just not open enough. In 2016 I turned to *liuhebafa* once more, but via a different lineage with a teacher named Nelson Ma 馬章英. Nelson is a native of Hong Kong living in the Vancouver area, teaching the complete *liuhebafa* system as passed on by Chen Yiren 陳亦人. His understanding of foundation training is profound, as well as his ability to work individually with students to change their body. He would also be a great guy to have your back in a bar fight! Although on the outside, *liuhebafa* could easily be mistaken for a dynamic form of tai chi, the internal principles of the art are quite different. Within a month of working with Nelson, my body began to open in a way never experienced before. It was a tough decision, but I chose to leave tai chi behind for good.

Before any of this happened however, I found what I was looking for: Taoist internal alchemy. I remember the week when everything changed. It was the spring of 2013, and I was finishing up a graduate seminar on *neidan*. Mulling over the previous week's readings on present day *neidan*, I was struck with a remarkable thought. If there are people teaching this stuff now, I mused, why not seek them out instead of waiting for them to come knocking on my door? Although I knew of a number of teachers in various locations around the globe, I had—for whatever reason—decided that they were not the real deal. I had built up a cynical voice in my head over the years which had conditioned how I saw these teachers. What was I doing? If I wanted to learn *neidan* then why not just go learn it? Then if the teacher was not what I wanted, at least I would know. And so, I consulted the great oracle of Google and compiled a list of active *neidan* teachers. Wang Liping was on that list.

Wang Liping

Austria changed my life. I arrived in August 2013, not really knowing what to expect. I was, at the very least, looking forward to visiting a lovely part of the world and maybe practicing some meditation.

The retreat was held in a cozy chateau just north of Innsbruck. I arrived a day early to get my bearings. When I saw Wang Liping coming down the stairs to the common room, I took the chance to introduce myself as a prospective student and a hopeful participant in the upcoming intensive. He appeared surprised—not only to encounter a white guy speaking Chinese, but also to see a new face. For one thing, Wang Liping does not bother himself with the administrative details of the various seminars he leads around the world; his students organize these matters so that he can focus on teaching. For another, this particular intensive was for more advanced students, people who could sit for at least two hours in duration. But there I was in the middle of it all.

My first impression of Wang Liping was of twinkling eyes and rosy cheeks. I know, I can imagine you rolling your eyes and thinking, "but that's how every high-level Taoist practitioner is described." To be sure, there are certain signs to look for in a Taoist master's appearance, including bright eyes, rosy cheeks, and clear, creamy skin. But that really was my first impression.

What I did not expect was his nonchalance. Wang Liping does not put on any airs; he is very candid and a little rough around the edges. When you speak to him, there is an intimacy; he feels like an old friend who knows everything about you. He also likes to joke around a lot and keep the atmosphere light. He does not seem to care for serious or intellectually-heavy conversation, and that is all I knew coming out of eight years of university. What a breath of fresh air.

Wang Liping invited me to join the group. The intensive started the next day, on a Friday, along with the most intense period of training I had ever encountered.

Austria, September 2013

The intensive was, to put it mildly, intense. The 12 of us assembled twice a day for a talk and a group *neidan* session. The sits, which we were expected to complete without moving, were geared for more advanced students and ranged in length from two to three hours each. On top of that, we participated in a myriad of other daily practices commencing with Taoist Walking at 6 a.m., continuing with tree practice at 8 p.m., and concluding with additional independent practices that lasted well into the night.

For me, things really started to move forward on the third day of the intensive, on Sunday, after Wang Liping mentioned that physical issues can arise from unresolved past life events. I found this interesting because of the pain I was experiencing in my right hip. Even though I had never injured my right hip, it had always been much less flexible than my left, and when I sat cross-legged it was always high off the floor. An experience I had that night clarified my hip pain.

Sunday night, I did my first mirror practice. Mirror practice is a special Taoist training method that involves meditating in front of a mirror, something I do not recommend trying at home without prior training. I dimmed the lights, calmed my mind, and carefully followed Wang Liping's instructions. In the darkness, my mind was able to project onto the mirror's murky surface. After about 45 minutes, the room suddenly became very still and I heard a distinct buzzing in my ears. I saw a fleeting image in the mirror and, for a brief instant, the side of a white horse.

In that moment, I had a choice: dismiss the phenomenon as a figment of my imagination or pay attention. I chose the latter, focusing on the image and feeling a rush of shivers shoot up my spine. As the drama unfolded before my eyes, I relived the emotional anguish of a tragic and bloody battle during which my right hip was crushed beyond repair. Because of the specifics of the drama involved, I made some decisions about myself that turned into ground zero for lifetimes of karmic crud to accrue.

After viewing the scene, the pain in my hip slowly began to release, moving through my body in an upward trajectory over the course of several days. It migrated to my left hip, then moved between my kidneys and up my spine, through my mid-back and chest area, and finally up my neck to the top of my head before releasing through my eyes and nose.

Twice during the process, Wang Liping helped move it. The first time was when the pain reached the area between my kidneys. During a *neidan* session, Wang Liping came up behind me and ever so gently stroked the area. The effect was immediate: a flood of raw emotion erupted out of me like a dam bursting, releasing unprocessed grief from a traumatic childhood experience. I pity anyone who had the misfortune of sitting next to me during that session. The second time was when the pain reached the top of my head. Wang Liping made some small movements with his fingers an inch above my head, once again releasing a torrent of pent-up emotion.

I continued working with the mirror throughout the intensive. On Monday night, I entered my dorm as usual, dimmed the lights, and followed the guided instructions that Wang Liping had shared with us. This time, my sit was interrupted by a voice in my head asking me for help. I was nonplussed. The first style of meditation I had learnt was from a Chan Buddhist lineage, known in Japan as Zen. This lineage teaches us to ignore any experiences we have during meditation by recognizing them as illusions, letting them pass, and continuing to sit. So, when confronted with a disembodied voice requesting help, I responded like any good Chan Buddhist: by ignoring it.

The next day, I told Wang Liping what happened. He looked at me and laughed. "When you have guests," he said, "don't ignore them. Talk to them." He explained that by paying attention to phenomenal experiences that arise during practice, we learn about the self; by learning about the self, we become free of it. That night the voice returned. This time I greeted it. It introduced itself as my brother—something I immediately dismissed as a lie. It apologized and said it needed help: it was stuck in a dark place and unable to get out. The only thing I could think to do was tell it to go toward the light—to look for a little bit of light and follow it. The voice never returned.

After I arrived home, I did not practice for a month. The Austrian intensive had been a bit overwhelming, and coupled with jet-lag and the challenge of reintegration back into normal life, I needed a little time off. Early in the intensive, a vibration filled my body. It had a buzzing character that was different from the feelings of *qi* that I had experienced previously, and during my first session back home, the vibration appeared again. It returned as soon as I crossed my legs, filling my body as though I had thrown a switch. I found this impressive. In my previous 15 years of working with *qi*, I had found that my practice needed to be attended to everyday. If I missed a day the *qi* quickly dissipated. Practicing with Wang Liping was different: the vibration remained even after a month away from practice.

Fall, Winter, and Spring 2013/14

After my first intensive, I took a year off of graduate school to work on *neidan*. I had fallen in love with the practice and wanted to give it my full focus. The plan was to return to university the following year to finish my MA thesis on *neidan*. I never did go back. I ended up practicing *neidan* full-time for three years, only slowing down when Darcy, my son, was born. For those three years, I withdrew from society, simplified my life, and practiced. With the exception of a ten-month gap between my first and second intensive, I attended one every three or four months. Each day I would practice for several hours, balancing one or two sessions of *neidan* with a session of internal martial arts. It was a lot of hard work but also a lot of fun. I finally felt like I was on the inside. After 15 years I was finally learning the secret, indoor methods of Taoist cultivation. I'd found the door and was finally invited inside. The irony is that the door was there unlocked all along. I just didn't have the courage to enter.

Twice a week, I attended one-on-one classes with my Wu family tai chi teacher studying indoor Wu family Microcosmic Orbit training (*xiao zhoutian* 小周天). Working with the Microcosmic Orbit involves opening the energy channels up the spine and down the front of the body. There are a number of cosmic orbits in Taoist practice, each of which works with different kinds of *qi*. Cosmic orbit practice is not usually a central part of tai chi practice, but the Wu family incorporated a version of the practice into their curriculum via a Taoist source some time ago. It presents an interesting example of how Taoist practice has influenced martial arts.

The Microcosmic Orbit I was learning manipulates the subtle tissues of the spine to open the channel. It is an extremely difficult practice involving the subtle and exacting movement of each vertebrae. Over the course of my study, I learned how to create space inside my torso and move my awareness inside my body. These skills are essential to *neidan* practice and they helped dramatically with what I started learning from Wang Liping.

After the Austrian intensive, my right hip continued to change. It opened up considerably, and when sitting cross-legged, my right knee was closer to the floor than it had ever been before. However, my hip was still tight. In search of a solution, I ended up at the door of my chiropractor, Dr. Shamira Rahim, who is also a Sufi shaman of sorts and who, over the years, has been instrumental at keeping me aligned in more ways than one. Shamira found a deposit of scar tissue around the femur head of the right hip joint. I had never injured it before; nevertheless, there it was. I committed to a series of laser treatments to break down the scar tissue.

During this time, I continued to work through the turbid *qi* (*zhuoqi* 濁氣) connected with the past life regression I experienced in Austria. Right after the intensive, a few of us took the train from Innsbruck to Vienna with Wang Liping. During the journey, Wang Liping talked with me about my past life experience, declaring that I would only be free of its karmic by-products once I was able to view the battle in its entirety.

So that autumn, along with the laser treatment and a conscientious stretching regime, I worked through the entire scene little by little. Six months later, I had observed the whole battle scene and released the turbid *qi* associated with the event. I was also enjoying a full range of movement in my hip, and I could even sit in half lotus during my sessions, something I had never been able to do before.

In the spring of 2014, I also began shaking. At some point in almost every session, I would tremble uncontrollably. The movements were powerful: some days my shoulders or torso would shake violently; other days I would rapidly bounce up and down. This lasted for a couple of years.

Turbid *Qi*

Taoist alchemy is not all fun and games. At times it can be tiring, uncomfortable, or even downright nasty. One of the challenges is sitting through the long sessions without moving. In order for our *qi* to transform, we must maintain our position, and sometimes this can hurt. If you do not like pain, you might be better off avoiding Wang Liping's method in favour of other more comfortable approaches to Taoist practice.

Another nasty aspect of the training involves purifying turbid *qi* (*zhuoqi* 濁氣). In order to undertake the alchemical work, we need to clean out the accumulated emotional and mental garbage locked in our bodies. Psychologists might call it unresolved trauma, but from the Taoist perspective it is dark, opaque, stuck *qi*. This kind of *qi* gets in the way of the alchemical work. It is hard to feel our subtle energy body if it is submerged in a cesspool of crud.

We acquire turbid *qi* with every stressful situation we experience. It accumulates whenever we are unable to process what is happening cleanly and clearly, we react from a place of "something is wrong," or we resist the moment. If someone cuts us off in traffic and we get annoyed, *qi* lodges in our system. If we do not completely process it, our body holds onto it. Mind you, a little road rage is not a big deal. Losing a loved one or surviving serious abuse leaves a much larger accumulation of turbid *qi*.

Cleaning out turbid *qi* uncovers one of the most difficult aspects of Taoist training. It is both life changing and demanding. There are many ways to process turbid *qi*. The traditional way is to undertake a process known as repentance training (*huiguo* 悔過), a method of moving the *qi* that holds us to the past. Working with the practices in this book will serve the same purpose. Learning the practices is easy. The challenges arise when we must face something again that we initially resisted many lives ago because of its complexity and pain. We do not need to go looking for turbid *qi*; it will come up naturally through the practice. All we need to do is be open to the experience. But that is the hard part.

Turbid *qi* can lodge deeply in the physical body, and its removal can be accompanied by a host of physical reactions, including chronic fatigue and various levels of sickness. As previously mentioned, I was not the healthiest person as a child or young adult. In the West we might say I had a weak constitution. A doctor of classical Chinese medicine, in contrast, would say that I was deficient in original *qi*, which is not a great diagnosis for a career in *neidan*. After my first intensive with Wang Liping, I was not sick for three or four years. I was often quite tired from the training, but I became quite immune to commonplace colds and flus.

Then one day I discovered a well of turbid *qi* that was locked away in my body, another layer to a traumatic experience I'd had when I was young. I could feel the *qi* release in a palpable manner. Two days later, I contracted a severe chest cold with a sore throat, congestion, coughing, and phlegm. I was bedridden for a month, and after that the cold returned every few weeks for over a year. Some of my students have struggled with the same thing. It is a challenging part of the training, especially when our modern lives are already so busy and hectic. My advice is to keep in mind that the turbid *qi* is finite and each time we move it our lives will improve.

Southeast Asia, July and August 2014

During my first intensive in Austria, I had the good fortune of meeting BK Wee and his daughter Xiaoling. They are close students of Wang Liping and served as translators for the event. BK had kindly invited me to a 21-day retreat with Wang Liping the following summer, which is how, in July 2014, my wife, Michelle, and I found ourselves on board a plane for Southeast Asia. I prepared all year for this event, slowly pushing the length of my sits until I cried out in pain and attempting, unsuccessfully, to activate my *xiatian* 下田. The *xiatian* (sometimes called Lower Dantian) is an energetic space in the middle of the lower abdominal cavity. I am sure my wife, Michelle, wondered the whole time what I had gotten myself into. Nevertheless, she never once wavered in her support of my practice. I am truly blessed.

The Southeast Asia intensive was a fasting retreat. Fasting empties out the physical body and allows us to tune into the energy body with more ease. It was there that I felt my *xiatian* for the first time, giving me my first real taste of what *neidan* has to offer. The *xiatian*, in the centre of the lower abdominal cavity, is an important energetic locus of the alchemical work, and discovering it is the first major benchmark along the path of alchemy. The interesting thing was that during the same sit, I also felt my middle field. Following Wang Liping's instructions, I was able to merge the two fields, moving the *qi* from the middle field down the internal centreline (*zhongzheng xian* 中正線) of my torso into the *xiatian*. When the two energy fields merged, my entire body exploded with light, warmth, and vibration. Each field vibrates at a different frequency; putting them together brought a powerful new resonance.

As these vibrations subsided, my awareness of my *xiatian* diminished as well. It took me several months to consistently tune into it again. Even though I worked diligently, I could not hold onto the movement of the field for any length of time. It is a slippery devil. To feel it, you need to be very stable and still. Even just breathing a little too loud will drive the awareness away. It took several months and at least two more intensives with Wang Liping before I could finally sense the *xiatian* without much work. After this intense process, the alchemical work became more accessible because I could focus on something specific.

The light of our spirit, or *shenguang* 神光, appears in front of our eyes when we practice, and seeing it is another benchmark for alchemical work. I saw mine during the Southeast-Asian intensive shortly after encountering my *xiatian*. I was in a session with Wang Liping and I could feel that my body was not completely sunk down. I relaxed my upper back while keeping a bit of my awareness on the *xiatian*, and as my body stabilized, I entered a deeper level of stillness. Suddenly I felt a rush of shivers up my back and a light about the size of a dime appeared before my eyes.

It hovered in front of me, pulsing to the movement of my *xiatian*. Unfortunately, I became excited, telling myself, "I see it, I see it!" The light vanished, not to be seen again for months. Lesson learned: curb the excitement Nathan.

On the same intensive, I experienced a dramatic opening of my Microcosmic Orbit, which includes meridians that lead up the back, follow the spine, and return down the front of the body. It can be opened in different ways, depending on the type of *qi* that cycles through it. In Southeast Asia, mine opened with hot *jing* energy 精, the densest form of energy in the body, and the energy most closely associated with the physical body.

Just as there are different ways to open the Microcosmic Orbit, there are different ways to mobilize *jing*. In Southeast Asia, my access point was pain. Pain is common when practicing Taoist alchemy with Wang Liping. When it arises in a session, it is a sign of energetic transformation or *qihua*. Change is good; we practice to transform the self. Wang Liping encourages us to endure until the *qi* changes.

During one memorable sit, I could maintain my focus until the pain in my legs penetrated the centre of my thighs to the bone marrow itself. This was hot *jing*. It had an intense, tingling sensation, and as it moved it felt like a viscous liquid inside my bones. As it migrated along the inside of my thigh bones toward my sit bones, it brought searing pain, and as it rose up the inside of my spine, my tailbone became numb. Skipping my lower back, it eventually re-emerged between my shoulder blades and continued its upward trajectory into my neck and head. By this time, it wasn't burning, just hot intense tingling. When it arrived at the top of the head, I felt an intense pressure on my *baihui* acupoint (百會穴), the highest point of the head. I could hardly keep my neck straight from the strain. My whole body felt like it was going to crumple. In agony, I moved my legs. Immediately the sensations stopped, like unplugging myself from an electrical socket.

The retreat in Southeast Asia was incredibly hard work. Training with Wang Liping is tough at the best of times, but fasting took things to a whole new level of difficulty. There were times when I wanted to quit, but I kept going. There were times when I swore I would never do another intensive, but I kept signing up. The hard part about fasting was that we maintained a full training schedule. The sessions were long, too, with sits ranging from two to four hours. But the results from the practice were significant. Sometimes we need to tear ourselves down before we can build ourselves up.

Continued in Chapter 16.

PART TWO

Theory

This glossary is repeated at the end of the book for easy reference.

Essential Terms for Practice

The following Chinese terms are the basic vocabulary needed to follow the practices in this book.

Jīng 精: literally essence; energy associated with our physical body.

Nèidān 内丹: literally translates as internal cinnabar. Usually translated as internal alchemy. Note: there are several names for internal alchemy in Chinese.

Qì 氣: energy or life force
   Qì 炁: the *qi* we make in our body

Shén 神: literally spirit, the high-frequency energy of conscious awareness.

Shénguāng 神光: light of our spirit; spiritual illumination. The *shenguang* plays an important part in our practice and will be discussed more in later volumes. Because we use it during the opening of our *neidan* sessions in this volume, it is included as essential vocabulary.

Xiǎofù 小腹: the lower abdominal cavity, situated below the navel and housing the Lower Space 下空.

Xiàtián 下田: literally translates as Lower Field and commonly referred to as the Lower Dantian. An important energy centre, and a main focal point during the first phase of the alchemical work.

Yìniàn 意念: a combination of awareness and intention.

Zhōngtián 中田: the Middle Field, commonly referred to as the Middle Dantian. This energy centre is in the middle of the chest cavity.

3.

Neidan Theory

This chapter introduces the basic theory of Taoist practice. In the old days, this theory would be shared after the fact, after success in practice. It would help contextualize the practice, making sense of what we have already experienced, as a map of territory already traversed. Do not confuse the map for the real thing. This chapter is not real Taoist knowledge; it merely contains some concepts to help us undertake the important task—the practice.

This book outlines a practice, encapsulated within a set of methods and techniques, that aims to change the self. This practice is an embodied experience, like swimming or riding a bike. We practice with the aim to experience a certain feeling. The feeling of balancing on a bike cannot be explained easily, but it is unmistakable. The same is true for Taoist alchemy; we practice until we get the feeling of it. Most kids do not learn how to ride a bike by reading about it.

When I first learned to ride a two-wheeler, my dad would run along behind me holding the back of the seat to make sure I did not fall over. Taoist alchemy is transmitted in a similar manner: the teacher shows us how to get on the bike, puts a helmet on our head, gives us a few short instructions, and off we go. Theory is not essential to the process. The essential part is the feeling, the knack—something not a teacher, a book, nor all the discussion in the world can give us.

Still the mind, find knowledge in the body.

Taoist alchemy refers to two things: Taoist cultivation (*xiudao* 修道) and *neidan* 內丹. Taoist cultivation is about returning to the *dao* 道. *Dao* literally means way. However, the *dao* cannot be conceptualized; it is beyond the limits of language. The *dao* needs to be experienced. *Neidan* is a tool to help us do that. *Neidan* refers to the methods and techniques that we use to create either a Golden Elixir (*jindan* 金丹) or the Sacred Embryo (*shengtai* 聖胎). However, it is not necessary to master *neidan* in order to return to the *dao*; it is merely helpful.

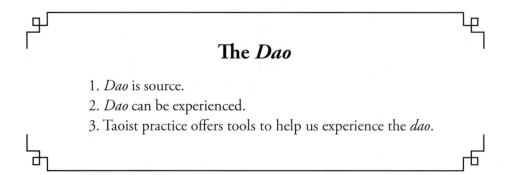

The *Dao*

1. *Dao* is source.
2. *Dao* can be experienced.
3. Taoist practice offers tools to help us experience the *dao*.

Even though the *raison d'etre* of Taoist practice is to return to the *dao*, the concept of the *dao* itself can be a little abstract. For this reason, Taoist cultivation is tightly bound with the cultivation of *qi* or energy—in fact, the more I practice Taoist alchemy, the more I appreciate the all-encompassing role of *qi*.[1] For practitioners, the actual nature of *qi* is not important. We can simply view it as a life force within our physical body, something we can work with directly, something that we can learn to experience and use.

We see, hear, and feel *qi* by way of the body. For this reason, the physical body is not only the foundation of Taoist practice, but also the gateway to the energy body. As we practice, we direct our focus to our body, which in turn gives rise to knowledge. From the Taoist perspective, this kind of knowledge is true knowledge, but it takes time and effort.

The Taoist alchemist recognizes different types of *qi* within the body, the most important include the internal Three Treasures (*sanbao* 三寶) of *jing*, *qi*, and *shen*. Just as ice, water, and steam represent different states of the same substance, *jing*, *qi*, and *shen* represent different forms of *qi*, all of which exist on a spectrum of density within the body, *jing* 精, literally essence, is the densest and the form most closely associated with our physical body. *Qi* is in the middle of the spectrum, not as dense as *jing*, but not as rarified as *shen*. *Shen* 神, literally spirit, is the most rarified and the form most closely associated with our awareness. The goal of *neidan* is to refine *jing* into *qi*, to refine *qi* into *shen*, and finally to refine *shen* to realize emptiness and return to the *dao*. It is an ongoing process of energetic transformation (*qihua* 氣化).

Stages of Internal Alchemy Training

1. Building foundation
2. Refining *jing* into *qi*
3. Refining *qi* into *shen*
4. Refining *shen* to revert to emptiness
5. Refining emptiness to join with the *dao*.

---

1 In the early days of the Warring States period (475-221 BCE) the terms *qi* and *dao* were even used interchangeably.

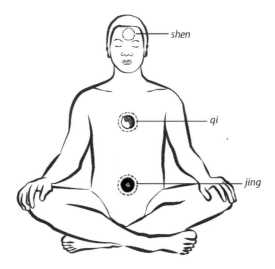

Jing, Qi, Shen

This book focuses on the first two stages of building foundation and refining *jing* into *qi*. Refining *jing* into *qi* cumulates with forming the Lesser Reverted Elixir (*xiao huan dan* 小還丹). The Lesser Reverted Elixir is a sphere of *qi* we form in the centre of the lower abdominal cavity. The process requires us to energetically seal the body, collect the alchemical ingredients (also known as the Medicine) from the body, deposit the *jing* into a space at the centre of the lower abdominal cavity known as the *xiatian*, and fire it to refine the *jing* into *qi*. Once this process is complete, we will have the Lesser Reverted Elixir.

The process of forming the Lesser Reverted Elixir is all about *qi*. *Qi* is subtle, however, and in the beginning it can be tricky to grasp. To work with *qi*, we need to develop a high level of sensitivity. One point of access is through *yinian* 意念, which is best translated as a combination of awareness and intention. *Yinian* is the single most important tool in our toolbox, and if we use it correctly, the classics say it will turn stone into gold.

Yinian is actually made of two interrelated aspects: *yi* and *nian*. I translate *yi* as intention: it is active; it has direction and movement; it is the *yang* aspect of *yinian*. *Nian*, conversely, is a passive field of awareness, embodying the *yin* aspect of *yinian*. We cannot separate *yi* and *nian*; they are *yin* and *yang* aspects of the same greater whole.

Yinian is easy to use, but hard to use properly. As with most things, the more we practice, the better we get. To use *yinian* properly requires focus. We still our mind, disperse our random thoughts, and focus on something. Try it now. After you finish reading the instructions in this paragraph, look up from the words you are reading and focus on something in the distance. Now your *yinian* has an object.

Ask yourself, what does it feel like to focus on a distant object? Now, bring your *yinian* to your hand. Does that feel different?

Yinian likes to have an object to attach to. This is normal. However, often during practice we are required to focus in the middle of an empty space. This is harder. Try it now: look up from the book—I will assume you are inside a room—and focus your *yinian* on a corner of the room that you can see. How does that feel? Now focus on another visible corner. How does that feel? Now without turning around and looking, focus on a corner behind you. How does that feel? Try another unseen corner or aspect of the room. It is harder to focus on what we cannot see. Now try focusing your *yinian* in the middle of the visible room. Not on the wall, floor, or ceiling, but in the open air in the middle of the room. Even though the space is visible, this step is harder because there is nothing for the *yinian* to attach to. This is how we use *yinian*.

Yinian does not work alone. When we focus on an object, energy goes along for the ride. This energy is *shen*. *Yinian* and *shen* are closely related. *Shen* gathers around the focal point of our *yinian*. Through practice we can increase the amount and clarity of our *shen* because *shen* is a substance. Paying attention to how we feel when using *yinian* is helpful for tuning into our *shen*.

Shen is a core component of Taoist alchemy. We use it so frequently throughout the alchemical process that *neidan* is sometimes known as a form of *shengong* 神功 or *shen* work, in the same way that qigong is referred to as energy work. But the cultivation of *shen* requires a foundation, without which the *shen* will not be full or clear enough to work with. *Shen* is delicate. Unless our mind and body are still and stable, it will easily disperse. We want it to quietly accumulate in our body, becoming thick and full as we focus inside during our practice session. We must be ever so careful and aware: even one wayward breath or movement can scatter it. When it comes back into our body, we say it has returned.

Because *shen* is connected to our *yinian*, it easily dissipates through our senses. From the Taoist perspective, our mind is a sense and therefore it too can play a role in dispersing our *shen*. Taoists call the *shen* associated with our senses: *shishen* 識神 (Spirit of Recognition). When we think or sense something outside of our body, even something far away, some of our *shen* goes there. Try it right now. Think of a friend you have not seen for a while or a room in your house you are not currently inside. Some of your *shen* will travel there immediately. Even thinking of past or future events will disperse your *shen* from the present moment. This is not a problem when the choice is a conscious one, even though most of the time it is not. Often, we are not even aware of our scattered *shen*.

Through our practice, we bring the *shen* back. We still the body and mind. As we focus inside the body, the *shen* begins to gather and pool, filling the inside of our torso, allowing our heart-mind to stabilize and the spirit to return. The more the *shen* gathers, the more *qi* and *jing* we will have. As we learn to contain our *shishen*, we also begin to transition into our *yuanshen*. *Yuanshen* 元神 (Original Spirit) is the opposite of *shishen*. *Yuanshen* is spirit uncontaminated by our this-world-physical existence. Abiding completely within our *yuanshen* is the goal of Taoist practice, and in the old days only by attaining this state was one worthy of the term *daoshi* 道士, or Taoist master.

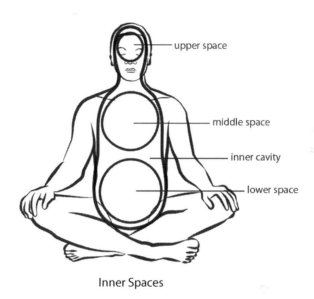

Inner Spaces

Now that we have gotten a handle on some of the basic tools in the Taoist alchemist's toolbox, let us look at where the work is done. Initially the laboratory is inside the body. The body can be split into three parts: the lower abdominal cavity, the chest cavity, and the head cavity. These three cavities are respectively known as the Lower, Middle, and Upper Spaces, and all three are collectively known as the Inner Cavity (*neiqiang* 內腔). Later in our practice, the Inner Cavity becomes central to our work, especially when using the Five Arts (*wushu* 五術).

Going through the centre of the Inner Cavity from top to bottom is the internal centreline (*zhongzheng xian* 中正線). The internal centreline rises inside the torso from the perineum to the top of the head. The line is not yet an energy channel. The practices in this book simply rely on the internal centreline for reference and orientation inside the body. Several of the lines used are unique to *neidan* practice. These lines are not found in classical Chinese medicine. Future volumes will explore the various lines inside the body and how to activate them. For now, it is enough to know the location of the internal centreline.

Usually we start working in the Lower Space (*xiakong* 下空) and progress upward in the body as we advance. The Lower Space is where our personal energy gathers. This is the energy associated with supporting our physical body and our individual survival. Sex, health, and personal power are all connected to the Lower Space. The majority of the practices in this book are focused on cultivating the energies of the Lower Space. By starting with the Lower Space, we ensure that we have the requisite health and power to continue along the way of our practice. Also, it's best to be well grounded when we start opening up the higher energy centres.

Xiaofu and *Xiatian*

In Chinese, we call the lower abdominal cavity the *xiaofu* 小腹. The area of the *xiaofu* is from the level of the navel down to the perineum. It may help to think of the *xiaofu* as a spherical space. In the centre of the *xiaofu* is the *xiatian* 下田. This smaller space, also spherical, is sometimes called the Lower Dantian 丹田, but within the Dragon Gate Lineage we only refer to a space as a *dantian* once it holds an elixir. The *xiatian* is the locus of the alchemical work. Often in deep meditation, we will focus on the *xiatian* and work to move, warm, or brighten its space. Much of our effort in this volume will revolve around finding and activating this energy centre.

This effort takes two forms: *youwei* 有為 and *wuwei* 無為. *Youwei* operates within the realm of intentional effort. We use it when our minds and bodies move in time toward a goal, when we actively engage with *neidan's* various methods and techniques. *Wuwei*, in contrast, involves letting things happen of their own accord. Stillness is a state of *wuwei*: we engage without controlling; we let things be. *Wuwei* is key: the first chapter of the seminal Taoist text *Daode jing* reminds us that "the sage inhabits a state of *wuwei*." While it can be helpful at times to employ methods (i.e., to use *youwei*), ultimately the real work happens in a state of *wuwei*.

The trick with alchemy is knowing when to do something and when to do nothing. For example, when we begin working with the *xiatian*, we alternate between *youwei* and *wuwei*. First, we put our awareness on the field and use intentional breathing to move it, regulating our inner breathing to guide its contraction and expansion. We also regulate the strength of our awareness. In essence, we do things; this is *youwei*. Then we forget the breath, forget the physical body, and observe the changes inside the body. If we are patient, the *xiatian* will begin to move on its own, eventually becoming warm and bright. But initially the *xiatian* is very delicate and needs to be nurtured with stillness. This is *wuwei*.

The language and metaphors of *neidan* can be overwhelming, but the basic terms and perspectives offer a helpful framework. In the next chapter, we will pay tribute to the importance of foundation, and after that we will be ready to start our work on the Lesser Reverted Elixir.

Taoism and Internal Alchemy

Taoism (or Daoism) refers to the constellation of Chinese spiritual teachings focused on returning to the *dao*, the source of our being.

Internal Alchemy is a tool to help us return to the *dao*. It is an esoteric form of Taoist mediation that is often shared privately between teacher and student. Internal Alchemy takes the body and its energies as foundation and leads the practitioner on a journey of self-knowledge and transformation.

4.

Foundation

Although my search for a teacher of *neidan* took a full 15 years, those years were far from wasted. The first Taoist lineage I studied did not teach classical internal alchemy *per se*, but they did have a deep practice with a solid understanding of foundation. Without those years of foundation work, it would have taken me a lot longer to make sense of what Wang Liping teaches.

Neidan is not an ideal introductory vehicle for Taoist cultivation. It is an advanced practice, requiring lengthy foundation work to prepare the body, mind, spirit and energy. Before the advanced energetic practices of alchemy can be successfully realized, the body and mind need to be conditioned. The body needs to be opened and strengthened, while the mind needs to be stilled and stabilized. Often foundation work takes years, but the good news is that pretty much any of us can undertake it, no matter where we live or our circumstances. Also, keep in mind, we do not need to complete our foundation training before starting *neidan* practice.

This chapter addresses two related but slightly different terms: building foundation (*zhuji* 築基) and foundation training (*jibengong* 基本功). Building foundation uses specific methods and techniques to insure there is enough *jing* and *qi* for *neidan* practice. Before looking at Wang Liping's way of building foundation, I will share the experience I have with Taoist foundation training in general. Even without access to a *neidan* teacher, we can work on our foundation.

A number of deep and profound practices are suitable for foundation training. Learning seated meditation such as silent sitting (*jingzuo* 靜坐) is ideal. Wang Liping's system of Taoist practice generally starts with silent sitting. Because *neidan* is primarily done in sitting meditation, we need to be comfortable sitting for long periods of time with legs crossed and mind focused. However, there are a number of other practices we can use for foundation training. My personal preference is

Chinese internal martial arts, but any mind/body exercise reaps benefits. Even if you do not have someone teaching you alchemy, foundation training can be found fairly easily, just walk into the local yoga studio or tai chi class.

Foundation training is something we work on throughout our practice. We continue to work on our foundation once we have started to practice alchemy. Likewise, we can start exploring alchemical methods before we have finished our foundation. Training is circular.

A good rule of thumb for alchemy is that foundation means being able to sit for four hours cross-legged with the body and mind relatively still. The bar is set quite high. In the old days the initiate would not start alchemy proper until they could achieve this level of foundation. That being said, I know from experience that we can reap results from *neidan* before hitting the four-hour mark. To sit for hours without moving requires us to tame our wild nature (*yexing* 野性), the part of us ruled by our senses and desires. The main desire here is, of course, to uncross our aching legs and do something else—anything else but sit and sit.

Mental Foundation

Sitting takes effort. It requires that we work not only our body but also our mind. But not just any work will do. Foundation of mind, also called stillness of mind (*xinjing* 心靜), is demonstrated by the ability to remain relatively undisturbed by internal or external stimulus. It is best achieved through silent sitting practice. If you want to practice *neidan*, but do not have access to a teacher, find a meditation teacher in the meantime. The whole alchemical project rests on a foundation of stillness. Learning to properly cross your legs and sit quietly in meditation is fundamental for *neidan* training and ideal for building foundation of mind. I studied Chan Buddhist (Zen) meditation with my first Taoist teachers and learned Tibetan Buddhist meditation in Taiwan. Both were immensely helpful for building foundation of mind.

Understanding and practicing stillness is essential for cultivating the *dao* in general and is no different when following the way of *neidan*. Both body and mind need to be as still as possible. As practitioners, it is up to us to figure out how to do this. Luckily, we have the experience of those who came before us.

The more we enter stillness, the more results our practice will produce. This is especially true when working with our subtle body or *dantians* 丹田, which must be approached in a state of *wuwei*. But what is stillness? It is, fundamentally, a feeling. When our mind is still, random thoughts slow down, move to the periphery, and perhaps even cease. When our body is still, we no longer move or make small micro-adjustments.

Movement can also arise out of extreme stillness. This kind of movement is beneficial, so allow it to happen in your practice. It may take many forms: in the body it may be *qi* moving or in the mind it may be inspired thought or a view of something far away.

Desire disturbs stillness. Our senses produce sensation, and sensation leads to emotion. In Taoist practice this phenomenon is known as the seven emotions and six desires (*qiqing liuyu* 七情六慾). Our senses create desire, and this desire disturbs our stillness.

The easiest way to hone stillness is just to practice it. Engage in your chosen activity, be it silent sitting or another form of stillness training (*jinggong* 靜功), and simply acknowledge any moments of agitation or unease. If you wish to take your stillness practice to a deeper level, other preparatory stillness practices for mental purification do exist.

One such method is called repentance (*huiguo* 悔過). Within the context of Taoism, repentance is a process of making peace with the past by releasing the turbid *qi* (*zhuoqi* 濁氣) that binds it to us. It is not approached through a moral framework but rather through *qi*. Turbid *qi* begins to build in our system from the womb. The more attached we are to our senses, the murkier it becomes. By cleansing our bodies of turbid *qi*, we are better able to calm our mind and enter stillness. In undertaking this process, we also begin to tame our wild nature, learning to control our emotions rather than allowing them to control us.

The Dragon Gate Lineage has several ways of practicing repentance. Here is the method Wang Liping followed with his teachers. The practice has three stages. The length of time required for each stage is dictated by the amount of turbid *qi* that needs to be purged. The first stage involves staying in a dark room for a few months with nothing for the mind to do. The second stage involves practicing silent sitting in this room, gradually increasing the length of each sitting session. During the third stage, the practitioner moves to a normal room. By this point each sitting session needs to be a least four hours long.

At the end of this process, the mind is relatively still, much of the turbid *qi* has been cleaned out, and the wild nature has been tamed. I have not gone through this training myself, and these days Wang Liping does not require it of his students. They start straight away with *neidan*.

When I started teaching, Wang Liping told me that it is best to teach various kinds of students differently. For example, how might we teach teenage as opposed to adult students, with their different life experiences and body types. One system of training does not fit all. Training is best tailored to each individual, and now in our modern world, repentance is often not a suitable way to start the practice. Nevertheless, foundation is still important, and it is up to each of us to understand what is required and take ownership of the process.

Physical Foundation

Physical conditioning is another important aspect of foundation training. A body-builder physique—with tight muscle definition and six-pack abs—is not what we are aiming for because it will severely limit what we are able to do with *neidan*. *Qi* needs to flow, and for this to happen, the deep tissues of the body must remain pliable. Taoist foundation training relaxes, engages, stretches, moves, and builds the entire body. This promotes a healthy, properly developed body free of stagnation. Even when we engage in static posture training, stilling the outside of the body, the inside remains in a state of movement. Movement equals health, stagnation equals illness.

On the most basic level, we need to be physically fit. *Neidan* requires long sitting sessions of intense focus. A lot of *qi* builds up inside and we need to be strong in order to hold it, especially when forming the elixir. Energetic transformation requires effort. If we are not physically fit, we will not be able to grow in the practice. There are many ways to get fit, but remember that we are not looking for exercise that develops isolated muscle groups or tightens the body. It would be preferable to find a personal trainer who can get you working on core-strength training or something similar.

Stretching is a great place to start work on our physical foundation. Opening the pelvis is vital for Taoist practice. When our pelvis is tight, our *qi* and blood circulation becomes restricted. The pelvic bowl is full of muscles, tendons and ligaments that need to be worked and relaxed for the pelvis to open. To open the pelvis, we stretch. Stretching has been a cornerstone of my practice since I started all those years ago. When we open the pelvis there is a feeling of space inside the pelvic area and sinking becomes possible (see boxed text on page 37: *Song and Sinking)*. All the sinews that go through the area become soft and pliable. Once the pelvis opens, the upper body and spine will also naturally become more relaxed and open.

To begin accessing the pelvis, stretch the legs. Many of the sinews that run through the pelvis attach to the upper legs and lower spine. Start with the legs, even just using some simple stretches to work the hamstrings. You will not regret it. Especially if you are male. Women have a much easier time with this part of the training. So, guys, if you want to do *neidan,* start stretching. Stretching is fairly easy to learn, just go down to the local gym, find a book, or poke around online. However, bear in mind that traditional Chinese stretching methods are different from modern Western approaches. The modern approach might be a good place to start, but it can only take us so far.

Another practice I highly recommend is fast walking. It's easy to do and good for your health. It gets our body, breath, blood, and *qi* moving; and movement, as we know, is key. When our legs move, our pelvis opens, boosting the flow of blood and *qi*. Also, fast walking moves the diaphragm and increases our lung capacity, allowing us to breathe better. Brisk walking is the basis of a supplementary *neidan* method called The Nature Energy Exchange Practice (*ziran huan qifa* 自然換氣法), commonly known as Taoist Walking (see Chapter 12).

My favourite method of foundation training is Chinese internal martial arts. Regardless of our philosophical position on self-defense, tai chi, *xingyi quan*, *bagua zhang*, and *liuhebafa* all work exceedingly well for foundation training. The downside is that each requires a lifetime of commitment to master, with gains taking time to manifest. On the other hand, each is deep and profound, constituting a fully developed system of practice in and of itself. As a teacher, I have found the best compromise is to select and employ specific martial arts foundation training sets (*jibengong*) specifically for the development of a student's foundation.

Chinese culture is also rich with various sets of movements for optimizing health. Approaches that incorporate *daoyin* (導引), qigong, or *neigong* training elements are beneficial for learning about energy and will lead toward a strong *neidan* foundation. Personally, I prefer a practice that first works the sinews and bones (*xingjin bagu* 行筋拔骨). Basic *qi* flows through the tissues of the body. Working the body ensures these *qi* circuits are properly grounded and insulated.

Working the mind is not enough. We also need a strong physical foundation to replenish *jing*, the energy connected to our physical body. A lack of *jing* energy is associated with physical depletion. Strong *jing*, on the other hand, not only improves your health, but also purifies our *shen*. In this way, mind, body, *jing*, *qi*, and *shen* are all connected. Practicing *neidan* is difficult if we are unwell; we first need to heal. From another perspective, that is what foundation training is all about: healing.

Song and Sinking

A crucial aspect of foundation training is learning to relax and sink. *Song* 鬆 means to release tension from the body. Sinking (*chen* 沉) is when the feeling of our body weight settles to the ground. In order to sink we first need to *song*.

Learning to sink is essential for *neidan* practice. Without sinking, we cannot ground the *qi*. If the *qi* is not grounded properly, problems may arise from our practice, especially when we begin activating higher energy centres. To hold the *qi*, we need to sink. Conversely, the more we sink, the more the higher energy centres will naturally open. But what is sinking?

When we learn to *song* and sink it feels like the flesh of our whole body relaxes and settles. The bones and structure of the body do not change much, but everything else sinks down. The whole body melts as all of the tension drains away, similar to a well-cooked chicken when the meat just falls off the bone. In *neidan* practice, we will feel the weight of our body descend onto our sit bones. Initially, most people will usually feel this is in the shoulders or chest. However, sinking happens everywhere. Even the eyeballs in their sockets can sink. We can always learn to sink more.

We can learn to sink with the *neidan* methods of pore breathing and the body squeeze, which are detailed in Chapter 6, Nine Basic Techniques, but foundation training will help immensely. When I look at a student to determine their level of physical foundation, I mainly look for their ability to sink. Interestingly enough, flexibility and the ability to sink are not the same. Flexibility is good. *Song* and sinking are better.

Building Foundation

Since most people are not aware of their *qi*, I have found—as a teacher—that engaging the mind and body serves as the best way to approach foundation work. Even if we are not practitioners, we are aware of our physical body and conceptual mind. These provide us with a starting point. *Qi* is more subtle. Working our body and mind is our way in, but it is not the end game.

Taoist practice at its core is about *qi*—energy. As discussed in the previous chapter, this *qi* can be sorted into three subcategories: the Three Treasures of *jing* (essence), *qi* (energy), and *shen* (spirit), all of which exist on a spectrum of *qi* from heavy to light. For *neidan* training, the more *jing*, *qi*, and *shen* there is in the body, the better. From the perspective of *neidan* practice, foundation training is done to replenish the Three Treasures. Working on our body and mind serve as a way to replenish our *jing*, *qi*, and *shen*. Increasing mental stability brings back and cleans our *shen*; opening and strengthening our body replenishes our *jing*. It is a cyclical process: working on *jing* and *shen* can both increase *qi*, and *qi* in turn purifies *shen* and replenishes *jing*. Different lineages of *neidan* go about this process in different ways. Some start with the body to increase *jing*, some start with the mind to return and purify the *shen*. Wang Liping's lineage generally starts with the latter. The take-away point here is that a good foundation requires both.

The Dragon Gate Lineage also contains specific preparatory methods for foundation training called building foundation (*zhuji* 築基). Building foundation ensures we have enough *jing* and *qi* to begin the alchemical work. Wang Liping's lineage generally starts students with silent sitting to still the mind and return the *shen*. Once the *shen* returns to inside the torso, *jing* and *qi* will begin to replenish. To do this, we apply the Yinxian Methods (*Yinxianfa* 引仙法). Yinxian Methods are part of the oral transmission of the Dragon Gate Lineage, and are used to restore us to our original healthy state, repair energetic leakages, and build foundation. There are 12 Yinxian Methods and within each method are numerous techniques. I have selected the most useful of these techniques for this book (see Chapter 6). Applying the Yinxian Methods helps us to build foundation.

Building foundation is not something we only do once in the early stages of our practice. *Zhuji* is something we apply in every session. In the early days of our practice, we may use methods to build foundation exclusively, but throughout our *neidan* practice, we constantly rely on building foundation. We use these methods in every session to prepare the body. For example, if we wanted to refine some liver *jing* into *qi*, we would start with building foundation in the liver to consolidate the *jing* before converting it. There is a common misconception that the stages of *neidan* practice are approached in a strictly hierarchical manner. Although there is a general trajectory to the practice, we can always circle back to work on earlier stages when needed.

Success with Taoist alchemy requires foundation. Although there are many reasons that we do not get results with *neidan*, the most common involves a lack of foundation. This chapter provides a large-scale overview of foundation practice. Use it. If you are new to Taoist practice, let this chapter serve as a roadmap of your journey's first steps. If you are a seasoned practitioner, use it to identify any missing elements in your practice regimen. Foundation training is an ongoing multi-dimensional process. Try not to overthink it. Just jump in and get going. If you have the opportunity to learn Taoist alchemy, seize it, even if your foundation is not where it needs to be. At the very least, you will gain from silent sitting. On the other hand, if you cannot find a *neidan* teacher, get to work on your foundation—even if only for a daily walk around the block.

PART THREE

Practice

5.

Stillness

Before starting *neidan* proper, we must work with the Yinxian Methods (*yinxian fa* 引仙法, see appendix 1). Done in sitting meditation, the Yinxian Methods form an essential compendium of techniques used throughout the alchemical process. The first of these, and also the most important, is Gather the Mind and Sit Quietly (*shouxin jingzuo* 收心靜坐)—the art of stillness.

Over the millennia, stillness has been a mainstay of Taoist cultivation. It is no different for *neidan*; stillness is the foundation upon which the alchemical project rests. It is where the magic happens. Without stillness of mind and body, our practice will not bear fruit. Stillness is not the end goal. Rather, it acts as a beginning point and baseline over the life of our practice.

Stillness, then, is where we start. In the Dragon Gate tradition, this involves simply sitting cross-legged without moving, staying focused for as long as possible. Although the method is straightforward, the practice is not. The mind and body like to move and holding them in a single position for extended periods of time takes resolve and practice: the mind gets bored and the body becomes sore and tired. Being able to still the mind and body is the first of many challenges on the path of Taoist alchemy. This barrier is known as the barrier of sitting (*zuo guan* 坐關). This chapter looks at the basics of Gather the Mind and Sit Quietly and gives us some tools to surmount this challenge.

Let us start by focusing on a single aspect of stillness: stability of mind. Our mind is still when our awareness can rest undisturbed by random thoughts. Random thoughts (*zanian* 雜念) include the inner voice and constant chitchat in our head. If right now you are thinking, *What inner voice?*, then that thought is the inner voice. The mind likes to move. Focusing on one thing for any length of time is not easy, but that is precisely what we want to do with this skill.

The easiest way to maintain stillness of mind is to give it an object upon which to focus. Like giving a noisy dog a bone, giving the mind a focus quiets it down, at least for a little while. The object can be almost anything, including physical sensations, energetic sensations, or the breath. The guided instructions will tell us where to keep our focus. If we are just doing silent sitting then it's best to keep our focus inside the body and observe. The longer we can manage this, the better.

Awareness is a translation of the term *yinian*, something we use throughout the alchemical process. Learning how to properly use *yinian* greatly helps us deal with random thoughts and enter stillness. In the first level of *neidan*, we aim to keep our *yinian* inside the body, and if not inside the body at least inside the the room in which we practice. When we think of something, our *yinian* goes to that thing. For example, if we think of our favourite frying pan, our *yinian* leaves our body and travels to it. This is very helpful when we are preparing breakfast, but not when we are forming the elixir. We want to keep our *yinian* in, or at least on, our physical body.

Here is a simple way to focus your *yinian* on your physical body. With your eyes closed and without moving, try observing your body's physical sensations. Then consider the following question: how do you know you have a body? Try it right now. The answer is that you can feel your body. You are aware of your body's tactile sensations. Use this tactile field as your object of focus. As the immortal Bruce Lee put it, "Don't think, feel!" There is no need to think about your body's sensations; just feel them. Try to observe your body without yielding to random thoughts.

Guided Instructions

Gently close your eyes
Focus on your body's tactile field
Without looking or moving, ask yourself how
    you know you have a physical body
Because you can sense it
Notice any sensations you have
Focus on the sensations of your body
Now the object of your attention is the
    sensations of your physical body
If your attention is diverted by random thoughts,
    bring it back
Maintain an ongoing flow of focus on the object
See how long you can maintain your awareness
    on the body

Another aspect of practicing stillness is the physical body. To cross the barrier of sitting (*zuoguan* 坐關), the body must be still. Learning how to regulate the body is vital to our *neidan* training. The second method of the Yinxian Methods is Regulate Body (*tiaoshen* 調身). Within this method are numerous techniques. Perhaps the most basic is do not move. If the body moves, your *yinian* and *shen* disperse. This brings us to the primary reason we work with stillness in Taoist alchemy: *shen*.

No talk of Taoist meditation would be complete without a discussion of *shen*. Stilling the mind is not unique to Taoist practice. It remains a staple of many other styles of meditation. *Shen*, in contrast, serves as a core characteristic of Taoist alchemy, and we will work with it throughout our practice.

Shen literally means spirit. It is a high-frequency energy associated with our mind but connected with our physical body. The challenge of working with *shen* is how it easily scatters when disturbed by an agitated body or mind. This is why we first bring our *shen* back to the body when undertaking alchemical work. *Shen* follows *yinian*, and by keeping our *yinian* focused on the body, we allow *shen* to return and gather inside.

Awareness and Intention

We work constantly with awareness in *neidan* practice, so let us explore what that term actually means from a Taoist perspective. Taoists spend a great deal of time researching *qi* and consciousness, and they have developed a fine-grained vocabulary for these concepts. For now, we will limit our discussion to one of the most basic forms of awareness: *yinian*, a combination of the interrelated aspects *yi* and *nian*.

Yi is intention. *Nian* is awareness.
Yi has movement and direction. *Nian* is a passive field.
Yi is *yang*. *Nian* is *yin*.

Yinian directs much of our *neidan* practice, especially at higher levels. First and foremost, we can use it to lead our *shen* and *qi*. *Yinian* is related to *shen*. *Shen* is a substance, the *qi* associated with awareness and intention. The *neidan* classics say that "when *yi* arrives, *shen* arrives; when *shen* arrives, *qi* arrives." When we hear a loud sound, our *yi* travels to that sound very quickly. Once our *yi* arrives, our *shen* begins to pool around the area where the sound occurred.

Try this. Look up from this book to a far wall. Now, while looking at the wall, clap your hands and notice what happens to your awareness. Almost immediately, *yi* arrives at the sound of your hands clapping. After a few moments, *shen* begins to gather at the same location. You can try this with other sounds in your environment. Ears focus faster than eyes, so you will always hear first and then look. *Yi* is connected with the ears and *shen* with the eyes.

Keep in mind that as we progress with our *neidan* practice, terms will shift, and the meaning of *yinian* will change as well. But more on that in future volumes.

Sitting Position

Internal alchemy is best practiced in a cross-legged sitting position. Since we will be sitting for long periods of time, it is important to sit comfortably and correctly. Here are some tips for maintaining a proper sitting position:

- Sit on the floor. Cushions or mats are fine for beginning students. Try to refrain from using a chair, unless you have a medical condition or injury.
- Cross your legs in one of four ways (see below).
- With your sit bones firmly planted, adjust your body weight so that everything drops onto your sit bones.
- Keep your sacrum erect. Beginners tend to tilt the top of the sacrum backwards. Try to keep it perpendicular to the floor. This may take time to open up, so try not to force it.
- Place your palms face down on your knees, with your fingers spread open. This hand position is called the Peaceful Hand Form (*pingan shi* 平安式).
- Relax your shoulders, arms, elbows, wrists, and hands.
- Maintain a straight and centred spine.
- Keep your lips gently closed, your teeth lightly touching, and your tongue touching your upper palate.
- Gently tuck in your chin.
- Check that your head is not tilted backward.
- Relax your whole body, ensuring that it is stable and comfortable.

There are four different ways to cross your legs when you sit. Choose whichever one works best for you.

Legs open

1. Legs open (*san pan* 散盤). Knees are bent and legs are crossed in front of the body. This position differentiates itself from position 2, legs crossed, where one leg is placed in front of, rather than on top of, the other. This is a fairly relaxed posture and good for long sits. Small pillows may be placed under the knees for support.

Legs crossed

2. Legs crossed (*ziran pan* 自然盤). Knees are bent and legs are crossed in front of the body. The outer sides of the feet are on the floor.

3. Single bind (*dan pan* 單盤, or half lotus). Best learned in person with a teacher.

4. Double bind (*shuang pan* 雙盤, or full lotus). Best learned in person with a teacher.

It is not necessary to focus on your posture throughout an entire session. Rather, set it up at the beginning of the sit and refocus at the close. Try to maintain your posture throughout a session, but also try not to focus on it too much. As Wang Liping puts it, there is no need to sit prim and proper so try to keep it natural.

Unfortunately, Wang Liping does not support sitting in a chair. I realize it is difficult for some students to sit cross-legged. However, *neidan* is an embodied practice and the position of the physical body does matter. Crossing our legs when sitting helps to properly structure the body: the pelvic bowl opens, the lower energetic gates seal, and the spine extends upwards. Although some of my students have initially used chairs, I have always encouraged them to work toward a cross-legged sitting position. Stretching is a good place to start, but even something as prosaic as walking can make a huge difference. My experience is that our overall health and longevity is closely tied to the flexibility and openness of our hips and legs. If the sinews that run through the pelvic bowl tighten up, the internal circulation of blood and *qi* is severely hindered. It is up to us to figure out how to keep this area open.

Stillness is important. It is the starting point for Taoist alchemy, and we use it constantly throughout the alchemical process. Stillness is also the culminating method of our alchemical work. Once we have followed the instructions to form an Elixir or Embryo, we once again sit in stillness, allowing it to crystallize and mature. We call this bathing and cleansing (*muyu* 沐浴). Nourish the Heart-Mind to Bathe and Cleanse (*yangxin muyu* 養心沐浴) is the twelfth and final one of the Yinxian Methods.[1]

In Dragon Gate *neidan*, we employ stillness within every session. As we will see in Chapter 7, a *neidan* session is split into two parts. In the first part of a session, we actively apply methods and techniques. In the second part, we sit quietly and allow the alchemical process to unfold. Because we cannot think our way through the process, stillness helps to sidestep the cognitive limitations of our conceptual mind.

Bathing and cleansing similarly assists with the overall trajectory of the alchemical process. There is a saying that we work on the Three Immortals Practice (*sanxian gong* 三仙功, the main body of alchemical work) for nine years. In the tenth year, we bathe and cleanse, simply sitting in stillness and allowing our efforts to bear fruit. Perhaps the best way to conclude this chapter is to invoke Wang Liping. He once said, "the secret of Dragon Gate *neidan* is understanding how to use stillness and how to bathe and cleanse."

---

1   Yinxian Method #12 is sometimes also called: Embrace the Origin and Bathe and Cleanse (*baoyuan muyu* 抱元沐浴)

6

Nine Basic Techniques

To understand Taoism, we must experience it. To gain experience, we practice. To practice, we must use methods and techniques. Thinking can help orient us to these undertakings, but to find knowledge in the body, we need to move beyond our intellect.

This chapter introduces nine basic techniques that can aid us in working with the mind and body and support us in our alchemical work. I handpicked the techniques from a larger collection of methods and techniques known as the Yinxian Methods. Along with the Three Immortals Practice and the Celestial Eye Practice, the Yinxian Methods form the core of Wang Liping's Dragon Gate system of spiritual transformation (see Appendix 1). Although these techniques support beginning students, they also can propel the practice of advanced students. Training is circular. We can always brush up on the basics, even if we have been practicing *neidan* for years.

The Nine Techniques

1. Inner Seeing (Body Scan)
2. Natural Breathing
3. Nose Breathing
4. Pore Breathing
5. Body Squeeze
6. Inner Hearing (Heart)
7. Lower Abdominal (*Xiaofu*) Breathing
8. Inner Breathing
9. Lower Field (*Xiatian*) Breathing

The Nine Techniques are best learned one by one. Start with the first technique and make your way sequentially down the list. When I taught weekly classes, I would teach my students a technique every week or two, but this is not necessary. We can simply work at our own pace to develop The Nine Techniques. While the techniques can be employed separately, they are often used together. For example, when practicing pore breathing, we can first use our nose breathing or natural breathing to lead the body pores.

These techniques are usually practiced in a meditation session. We cross our legs, close our eyes, and follow the teacher's guided instructions. If you are following this book, start by memorizing the instructions. Although these techniques most commonly apply in a sitting position, you may also choose to practice them standing, lying, or walking. Once you get comfortable with them, you may find that you can practice them anywhere and anytime. Natural breathing, nose breathing, and even pore breathing can be done while you are waiting for the bus, sitting at a desk, or taking a brief respite from the various screens in your life.

How to use the Guided Instructions

Most techniques include a short introduction and guided instructions (*daoyin ci* 導引詞). The guided instructions, which have been passed down to us over many generations, were secret instructions that form the bulk of the oral transmission of the Dragon Gate Lineage. These instructions tell us how to do the technique. Here is a way to apply them to your practice:

1. Read them.
2. Memorize them.
3. Practice them, following the words in your head.
4. Embody them, transcending the memorized words
   and allowing the sessions to follow their own flow.

In other words, guide yourself with the memorized words until your body automatically knows what to do, at which point you may bypass the words.

Initially, sessions are fairly structured and repetitive. Instructions are repeated to allow you to hardwire the techniques into your body. Once you have embodied them, the sessions can begin to unfold by themselves. First, however, focus on structure.

1. Inner Seeing—Body Scan

We spend much of our daily life focused outward. Our senses are arranged to get information from around us, and they keep us safe, allowing us to function in the normal world. When practicing, we turn around our senses and focus on the body. The physical body is the basis of Taoist practice and the foundation of our self in this world. Inner Seeing is a useful means of reorienting us back to our physical body.

We practice Inner Seeing simply by looking inside our body. Despite the simplicity of the method, it is one of the most important tools we can use in the alchemical process. There are four types of seeing: Seeing Afar (*yuan shi* 遠視); Turn Around Observation (*fan guan* 反觀); Inner Seeing (*nei shi* 內視); and Inner Observation (*nei guan* 內觀). The key to using Inner Seeing correctly is to understand visualization (see boxed text on page 53: *Visualization*). The instructions tell us to turn around our observation and look within. Rather than simply focusing within yourself, I encourage you to approach the instructions literally. Something happens when we close our eyes and move our eyeballs to focus within, even though our eyes cannot see inside our body. By trying to look within, we open up a space for information to arise.

To use Inner Seeing, we will need something to look at, and in this case, the object of our focus is the body. Although Taoists recognize different types of bodies that comprise the self, this book will work mainly with the physical body divided into inside and outside. When scanning the inside, we generally focus on the Inner Cavity of the head, neck, and torso. When scanning the outside, we start from the skin of the head, chest, abdomen, and four limbs, and then work inward to the meat and bones. The external physical body is the easiest place to start.

The first stage of this technique is so simple that it is easy to miss. Simply close your eyes and look. That is all. Look at your head, chest, abdomen and four limbs. If you are new to this practice, feel free to use a little imagination. Imagine your external form in detail (the clearer the better). You want to create a well-defined image of your physical body in your mind. This requires that you focus your *yinian*. Bring your *yinian* back from wherever it went and put it on your body. If any random thoughts arise, just bring your *yinian* back to your body. Focus on the body. Think about the body. Imagine your outer physical form.

By doing this you bring your *yinian* and *shen* back to your body. Not only does this calm your mind by providing you with an object of focus, it also puts you in touch with your body, bringing you back to your body and making you happier and healthier. It is also a fundamental technique for later *neidan* practice.

Guided Instructions:

Look within, with eyes closed, look at head,
        chest, abdomen, and four limbs
Look at the shape of your external form
See it clearly and in detail; if you cannot see, imagine
Bring your *yinian* and *shen* back to your physical body
Let your body be relaxed, stable, and still

Now that your *yinian* is back in your body, let's
        look at the body in detail
Start with the top of the head
From the top of the head, slowly descend
        following the instructions
Strong awareness, relaxed body

Clearly see in detail the front, back, left, and right
The complete outside features of the body
        starting with the top of the head
Now move down to the level of the forehead
        down to the level of the eyes
        down to level of the nose
        down to level of the mouth
        down to level of the neck

The shoulders and upper chest
The shoulders and lower chest
The upper abdomen
The navel
The lower abdomen and hips
The thighs, the lower legs, the feet
The arms, elbows, wrists, hands, and fingers

See the body clearly and in detail
Notice the shape, colour, and brightness
Notice if some areas are clear or faded
Remember these details and put them in your heart
Now you are regulating the body
Let the body be relaxed, stable and still

Do silent sitting for as long as you like

Visualization

Intentional visualization is not a common feature of Wang Liping's lineage. When it is used, there is a distinction to keep in mind. There are two kinds of visualization: intentional and unintentional. We call visualization intentional when we consciously try to imagine something and unintentional when images spontaneously appear. Dreams are an example of the second kind of visualization.

Unintentional visualization is best. It is relatively passive: we open up a space and wait for an image to emerge. Intentional visualization can be useful at times, but it is good to be clear with ourselves that it is only imagination. Otherwise, we can fall into delusions about our practice.

When you first practice Inner Seeing, it is fine to use intentional visualization. Just keep in mind that you are using imagination to intentionally visualize. Also be aware of any images that come to you. Even though you are intentionally visualizing the physical body, the images that appear will not be completely conscious. At some point, the unconscious mind will begin filling in details. Let this happen.

It is best to allow the entire image to appear without conscious thought. This then becomes unintentional visualization. When this happens, pay attention to such details as shape, colour, and brightness, and note any gaps or omissions. Also notice how the image changes—not just in that particular session, but over days and even years.

Sometimes the line between intentional and unintentional visualization can be blurry. But with practice it becomes easier to tell the difference.

MINI PRACTICE

Close your eyes and think of your kitchen. Take note of whatever image appears, but do not try to fill in the details just yet. Simply pay attention to whatever comes to mind. Modern understanding dictates that we are accessing our memory. The Taoist perspective acknowledges memory, but also considers the process of seeing our kitchen differently. When we think of a place, a part of our *shen* actually travels there. Furthermore, the image that appears is not random, so it is crucial to note the details. Looking at our body is the same as looking at our kitchen.

2. Natural Breathing

Regulating our breath is another vital component of Dragon Gate *neidan*. The techniques contained within this method are legion. We will start with natural breathing (*ziran huxi* 自然呼吸), also called normal breathing (*fan xi* 凡息).

There are two kinds of natural breathing: unintentional and intentional (also called *youwei* and *wuwei* breathing). Unintentional natural breathing happens when we breathe without thinking about it. It just happens. Intentional natural breathing occurs when we begin to adjust our breath, perhaps making it finer, smoother, slower, or deeper. Note that the breathing does not have a focal point, purpose, or pattern. We are not, for example, focusing specifically on our nose or lungs. We are simply putting our awareness on our breath and regulating it. This is intentional natural breathing.

The most common way to regulate intentional natural breathing in *neidan* is to breathe fine, even, and long. This is a good baseline for our breathing before undertaking anything complicated. Let's take a look at the three instructions one at a time.

Breathe Fine

To breathe fine (*xi* 細) is to breathe in a controlled and subtle way. Fine breathing is not rough or forceful, but rather completely silent. If you can hear your breathing, then it is not fine. The more present and focused you are on your breath, the finer your breathing becomes.

Breathe Even

To breathe even (*jun* 均) is to breathe in a smooth, stable, and constant manner. Even breathing does not speed up or slow down. It is continuous. Initially it may be helpful to make the inhale and exhale circular, aiming for a smooth transition between inhale and exhale, and exhale and inhale.

Breathe Long

To breathe long (*chang* 長) is to slow down the breath, extending the length of inhale and exhale. Each breath should not only be as long as possible, but also as relaxed and easy as possible. If you feel like you are tensing up or gasping for air, you are slowing the breath down too much. Extending the breath takes time and practice.

A note about Taoist breathing: the chest should be relaxed. Generally, abdominal breathing is best. This means that the abdomen moves, not the chest.

Guided Instructions

Slowly put *yinian* on your breathing
Now intentionally regulate your breathing
First make the inhale and exhale even
Inhale and exhale evenly

Now regulate breathing to be fine
Breathing fine means the breathing is soft and delicate
The breathing is not rough or heavy

To breathe fine you must completely focus on
    your breathing
Follow the air in and out of your body
Do not change the breathing other than to make it fine
To breathe fine you need control and awareness
Fine breathing is silent breathing; although you are
    breathing you cannot hear your breathing

Breathe fine
Regulate your breathing to be fine
Notice the air coming in and out of your body
Focus on your breathing
Make the breathing soft and delicate
Now you are breathing fine

Now, regulate your breathing to be fine and also even
Breathing even means the breathing is smooth
    and constant
The breathing does not increase or decrease;
    it stays the same
To breathe even, you must focus on the complete
    cycle of your breath
Follow the breath as it changes from inhale to
    exhale and exhale to inhale
Make the breathing circular
There are no gaps
The breathing is even and smooth
Breathe even
Regulate breathing to be even
Notice the cycle of your breathing
Stay focused on your breath

Breathe even
Now you are breathing fine and even

Now regulate breathing to be fine, even, and also long
Breathing long means you slow down your breathing
The breathing is not short or rushed

To breathe long, you must stay very focused
Follow the complete cycle of your breathing
Slow down your breathing
The body must stay relaxed
Gently slow down your breathing
Now you are breathing fine, even, and long

Regulate natural breathing
Breathe fine, even, and long
Inhale and exhale evenly

Now regulate breathing to be very even
Slowly forget your breathing, return to normal breathing
Do silent sitting for as long as you like

3. Nose Breathing

Taoist alchemy uses an array of breathing techniques. It might be helpful to note that we are not actually changing the way we physically breathe. For the vast majority of these techniques, air still comes in our nose, goes down our throat, and fills our lungs. What distinguishes them is the object of our focus.

When undertaking nose breathing, focus our *yinian* on the nose. Although air is still coming into our lungs normally, direct our attention to the air going in and out of our nose, regulating gentle nose breathing. Stay focused on the nose. If any random thoughts arise, simply bring our *yinian* back to our nose. It may help to visualize the nose as well. With eyes closed we look within. Think of our nose clearly and in detail. Nothing else in the world exists but the breath going in and out of the nose.

There are three parts we can focus on while nose breathing: the tip of the nose, the openings of the nostrils, and the two nostrils themselves. You choose which part works best for you. As you progress, *neidan* practice becomes more specific, so keep it simple for now.

First, we will work on gentle nose breathing (*wenxi* 溫息, literally warm breath). This resembles natural breathing, but with an added instruction to breathe gently: soft and light. Breathe fine, gentle, and long. You should not hear the air coming in and out. Regulate your breathing so that it is silent.

Guided Instructions

Focus *yinian* on your nose
Look within, look at your nose
Regulate gentle nose breathing
Breathe fine, gentle, and long
Inhale and exhale evenly

Now you are breathing with your nose
If you have any random thoughts bring *yinian*
    back to your nose
Let nose breathing disperse any random
    thoughts in your mind or random
    thoughts in your body
This breathing is silent
Even though you are breathing, you cannot
    hear your breathing
Keep the forehead relaxed and open

Regulate gentle nose breathing
Breathe fine, gentle, and long
Inhale and exhale evenly
Do this as long as you like

Sealing the Seven Upper Openings

Here is a sub-technique to use with nose breathing. Once you have a handle on nose breathing, you are welcome to give it a try. Alternately, feel free to skip it for now and move directly to Pore Breathing.

While each of the nine techniques can be powerful practices in their own right, they are used to get things done within the broader context of Taoist alchemy. Before we can go inside the torso and begin the alchemical process, we need to close the various energetic openings and gates. We often use nose breathing to seal the sense organs in our head (*mingqiao* 明竅). The sense organs are known as the Seven Upper Openings: two eyes, two ears, two nostrils, and one mouth. They are openings from the inside to the outside of the body used to sense the world. *Neidan* works best when the openings are closed, allowing us to keep our senses and therefore our *yinian* inside our body. We call this putting the lid on the cauldron.

To seal the upper openings, focus some *yinian* on them while nose breathing and allow them to breathe with the nose. As air enters the nose, the eyes, ears, nose, and mouth ever so slightly contract inwards. As air exits the nose, the openings gently release. When it is working, you will feel a warm fuzzy or full sensation over the sense organs. This is *qi* sealing up the openings. This exercise works even better if you include pore breathing, which will be discussed next.

Guided Instructions

> Focus *yinian* on your nose
> Regulate nose breathing
> Breathe light, gentle, and long
> Inhale and exhale evenly
> Turn around observation and look within, look
>   at your nose
> Regulate nose breathing
> The nose is the centre point of the head
> As you regulate nose breathing, think of eyes,
>   nose, mouth, ears
> The seven upper openings
> Check that the seven openings are properly sealed
> Eyes must not look out
> Ears must not listen out
> Nose must not smell
> Mouth must be closed
> All seven openings are sealed

4. Pore Breathing

This is where the practice starts to get interesting. Pore breathing, *breathing* with the pores of our skin, is quite possibly the most useful foundational technique Wang Liping teaches. We use it a lot, especially in the early days of our *neidan* training. This technique is a little more complex than what we have worked on so far, so let's take our time and properly unpack it.

Before the alchemical work can be done, we need to stabilize the furnace (*anlu* 安爐). In phase one of *neidan* practice, the furnace is the physical body. Pore breathing energetically seals the body (*xiu bulou* 修補漏) and builds foundation (*zhuji* 築基). Pore breathing also begins working with *yin* and *yang* energy, and is the first *kan* and *li* practice we do in Dragon Gate alchemy (see Chapter 9).

Taoists see body pores as the boundary between the human universe and outside space. In the old days, pore breathing was called Personal Universe Breathing (*zishen yuzhou huxi* 自身宇宙呼吸). During most *neidan* sessions, we need to set up the human universe, in effect designating an inside and an outside space. Pore breathing assists with this process. Although no air is actually going in and out of our body pores, something is happening. The technique allows us to focus clearly on our physical body. When we practice the body scan, we build up an image of our external physical form. Now we are feeling the body, allowing it to subtly contract and expand with the breath. This not only feels great but also allows us to begin moving and working the whole body.

Pore breathing is a core technique for *neidan*. Practice it often. It takes time to figure out, so be patient, but keep in mind that you need not master it before moving on to other techniques.

Guided Instructions

> Look within, look at your head, chest, abdomen,
>   and four limbs
> Look at your external form
> Slowly bring *yinian* back to your body pores
> We have 84,000 body pores, the border of the
>   human universe
>
> Breathe in, body pores contract
> Breathe out, body pores expand
> Repeat this process 24 times
>
> Return to natural breathing
> Do silent sitting for as long as you like

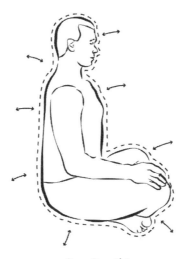

Pore Breathing

There are different dimensions or aspects to pore breathing. Start with the first two. When you feel comfortable with the practice, start adding in other aspects. There is no need to focus on all of the aspects at the same time.

Five aspects of pore breathing:

1. Focus: concentrate your *yinian* on your body pores
2. Breath: breathe in, contract body pores inwards; breathe out, expand body pores outwards
3. Move: let your body subtly move with your breath
4. Suck: encourage a subtle sucking and releasing sensation.
5. Split: intention on pores, awareness in space around body, anchor point in the body

1. Focus

Before starting pore breathing, focus your *yinian* on all of your body pores. The body scan works well for this. Remember, the various breathing techniques mainly differ in terms of where you place your *yinian*. Air stills goes in your nose to your lungs, but for body pore breathing, the focus is on your skin and external form.

2. Breathe

To do pore breathing, contract and expand your body pores with your breathing.

Guided instructions

Breathe in, contract body pores inwards
Breathe out, expand body pores outwards

Of course, you do not literally move each and every body pore. Instead, feel the entire surface of your skin contracting inwards and expanding outwards.

When you first start pore breathing, it is easiest to drive it with nose breathing or natural breathing. For example, you can start with nose breathing and then use the nose breathing to lead body pore breathing. You will need to split your awareness, focusing some on the air going in and out of your nose and the rest on your body pores. Start the inhale with your nose. Then quickly focus on sucking in with your body pores, so that you inhale with your body pores a fraction of a second after you inhale with your nose.

You may have noticed that this kind of breathing relies on something called reverse breathing: when we breathe in we contract, when we breathe out we expand (see boxed text on page 62: *Reverse Breathing*).

3. Move

Allow the body to subtly move with your breathing. Your body will squeeze just a little on the inhale and relax on the exhale.

4. Suck

Body pore breathing is often accompanied by a subtle sucking and releasing sensation. It may feel as though your body pores are sucking in something when you breathe in and releasing it when you breathe out. This something is *qi*—Pre-Heaven Original Qi (*xiantian yuanqi* 先天元氣) from the natural environment, to be precise. As your pore breathing develops, you may find that you are able to bring *qi* deeper inside your body on the inhale and expand it farther outside your body on the exhale.

5. Split

Another more advance aspect of pore breathing is learning to split your *yinian* (intention/awareness). Put some focus on the pores moving in and out with your breathing, while remaining aware of the space around your body, and finally anchoring your awareness inside your lower abdominal cavity. Splitting *yinian* is not easy, but with a little practice, it works wonders for our *neidan* practice.

To review, *Yinian* means awareness and intention together. *Yi* is intention. *Yi* has direction and movement, and is the *yang* aspect of *yinian*. *Nian* is a passive field of awareness, and is the *yin* aspect of *yinian*. Put *yi* on pores, where the movement happens, *nian* outside the body, and the anchor point inside the lower abdominal cavity (*xiaofu*). You may also use your *xiatian* as the anchor point if you are able. By splitting your *yinian*, you will learn to move *qi* more powerfully into and out of your body.

Guided instructions

> Breathe in, *qi* from all directions compress into
> whole body pores, and into *xiaofu/xiatian*
> Breathe out, *qi* from *xiaofu/xiatian* releases through
> body pores into surroundings

Reverse Breathing

Our body moves when we breathe. This is a complex maneuver; it involves contracting our diaphragm, which encourages all sorts of internal movement. When we first begin intentionally regulating our breath, we often learn to expand our belly and abdominal cavity. This works well for relaxing the body and pulling our awareness downwards from our heads. We can also reverse this way of breathing. Reverse breathing contracts our belly on the inhale and expands on the exhale. This type of breathing is often used in Taoist practice to achieve certain results. We do not do it all the time, but at certain times it is useful. Pore breathing is one of those times.

5. The Body Squeeze

The body squeeze, which teaches us to contract and expand the body with the breath, is in some ways a continuation of pore breathing. An easy way to start is to combine it with pore breathing by interspersing a body squeeze every four or five breaths. We can also practice it as a standalone exercise, but I suggest not doing it more than twenty-four times, unless it is of the soft and subtle variety.

There are a number of applications for the body squeeze. The practice relaxes and releases tension from the body. It creates space inside. It also helps us bring our *yinian* and *shen* into our body. Perhaps most usefully, it fills and smoothly distributes our *jing* and *qi* inside our body. When we get this practice right, the inside of our torso feels full and alive.

Guided Instructions:

Breathe in, whole body contract
Breathe out, whole body relaxes, body sinks down
Repeat

The body squeeze is not a subtle movement. When you contract, your physical body moves. Always end with an outbreath, allowing your whole body to release and relax downwards, sinking onto the sit bones. When this works, you will feel a subtle rise and fall. Contract and rise with the inhale; expand and sink down with the exhale.

Some aspects of the body squeeze are listed below. Start with the first. Once you feel comfortable, throw in another aspect. There is no need to focus on all aspects in the same session.

Aspects:

1. Contract your whole body inwards on the inhale;
   expand your whole body outwards on the exhale.

2. Relax your whole body, sinking down as you
   breathe out.

3. Explore the full range of contraction and expansion.

4. Stay gentle; squeeze your body subtly when you contract.

5. When you breathe in, allow your body to rise slightly.
   When you breathe out, allow your body to sink slightly.
   Keep your spine straight.

6. When you breathe in, allow the top of your
   thigh bones to contract towards your pelvis.
   When you breathe out, relax.

Play around with it. If you feel tense, anxious, or unsettled while doing this exercise, try approaching it in a more relaxed manner.

6. Inner Hearing

Taoist practice includes four main types of hearing: Far Hearing (*yuan ting* 遠聽), Near Hearing (*jin ting* 近聽), Return Hearing (*fan ting* 反聽), and Inner Hearing (*nei ting* 內聽). For now, we will focus on Inner Hearing, the sister skill of Inner Seeing. In *neidan* practice, the two are often used together. Inner hearing gives us another means of access into the physical body. We listen and observe within.

Inner Hearing is more than just a poetic term for focusing inside the body. As with Inner Seeing, I recommend approaching this technique literally. My own epiphany came with the realization that sound, movement, and feeling all interconnect. When we hear, the brain makes sense of the vibrations hitting our inner ear. Similarly, when we listen inside the body, we tune into its internal movement. The Taoists say that where there is movement, there is sound. The technique of Inner Hearing is a process of sensing the movement of our inner landscape.

There are many things we can listen to within the body. During the alchemical process, we will be called on to listen to specific areas, organs, or energetic phenomena. Different sounds have different volume. There are three main levels of noise within our body. The lungs and respiratory system are the loudest. The heart and circulatory system are quieter. The sound of the energetic system of our subtle body is the quietest. We can use Inner Hearing to listen to all of these.

To practice this skill, I recommend starting with the heart. The sound of our breathing is too easy; finding our heartbeat is trickier. Our ability to hear our heartbeat indicates our depth of stillness. Hearing our heart means our mind is still (*xin jing* 心靜); it is the first benchmark of success in Taoist cultivation. If you are not able to hear the heart, then use the sound of breathing as the object.

Inner Hearing

Guided Instructions

Use your inner ears to listen inside
Focus inside the body
Listen to your heart
The heart is a physical reality
The heart is moving, therefore the heart
    has sound
Listen to the sound of your heartbeat

If you cannot hear the sound of your heart,
    then stop breathing
Now you are not breathing
Listen to the sound of your heart
Once you hear the sound of your heart, once
    again start breathing
But make sure the sound of your breathing is
    not louder than the sound of your heart

Listen within, listen to the sound of your heart

7. Lower Abdominal (*Xiaofu*) Breathing

Next on our list of techniques is learning to breathe with our lower abdominal cavity (*xiaofu* 小腹). *Xiaofu* breathing is a powerful practice in its own right: it relaxes the body and the mind, brings more air into the lungs, and moves and massages the internal organs. These health results are an added bonus to the primary aim of abdominal breathing in *neidan* practice: to pressurize the Lower Field (*xiatian* 下田).

Taoist alchemists use *xiaofu* breathing to pressurize and control the Lower Space (*xiakong* 下空), the area of the lower abdominal cavity. At the centre of the Lower Space is another spherical space, the *xiatian* that will become a primary locus of our alchemical work. *Xiaofu* breathing is a means to work with these two areas.

The *xiaofu* extends roughly from the navel to the bottom of the torso, filling up the inner space. To breathe with this space, we contract and expand the outside of the lower belly with our inhale and exhale. We use reverse breathing: we breathe in, contracting the front of the lower belly inwards; we breathe out, expanding the front of the lower belly outwards. End the movement expanded and relaxed.

Explore the movement. Find the best way to contract and expand the *xiaofu*. Find the full range of movement. See how far the front of the lower belly will contract inwards. Try to keep the rest of the body relaxed. We have a tendency to tense other parts of our body when contracting anything. Attempt to localize the work as much as possible.

Do not be afraid to go deep. Once you become familiar with this breathing, see if you can make it move in a spherical manner. The sphere contracts and expands, following the breath inside the lower abdominal cavity. Remember that a sphere is a three-dimensional shape. To contract it, all directions compress inwards. To do this, slowly decrease external movement and slowly increase internal movement. The internal movement will be subtle. Try to avoid using the muscles to contract and expand; use *yinian* instead.

One final note. *Xiaofu* breathing, like pore breathing, derives from nose breathing, natural breathing, or inner breathing. Inner breathing is the next technique discussed below. Start with nose breathing. When you begin working with aspects five and six, switch to inner breathing. Remember not to work on all aspects at once because they get progressively more advanced, and there is no need to tackle them all right away.

Aspects

1. Focus *yinian* on the *xiaofu* area.

2. Breathe in, contracting the front of the *xiaofu* inwards; breathe out, expanding the front of the *xiaofu* outwards.

3. Find the full range of movement, whether large or small.

4. Seal the lower three *yin* gates (see below).

5. Move the Lower Space in a spherical manner, contracting inwards and expanding outwards.

6. Gradually make the physical movements smaller and smaller.

7. Eventually, just contract and expand inside, without moving the outside of the body.

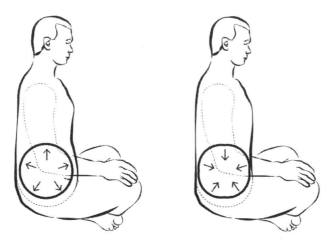

Lower Abdominal *(Xiaofu)* Breathing

Guided Instructions

Use gentle nose breathing to move *xiaofu*
Let *xiaofu* move with gentle nose breathing
When you breathe in, *xiaofu* contracts inwards
When you breathe out, *xiaofu* expands outwards
Use gentle nose breathing to move *xiaofu*
Let *xiaofu* move with gentle nose breathing

Breathe in, *xiaofu* contract
Breathe out, *xiaofu* expand
Repeat 24 times

Now regulate your breathing to be very even
Slowly forget your breathing, return to normal breathing
Relax whole body, body sinks down
Do silent sitting for as long as you like

Sub-Technique: Sealing the Lower Three Yin Gates

Once you are comfortable with the *xiaofu* breathing, try energetically sealing the bottom of the torso. Breathing with the *xiaofu* presents a great opportunity to seal up our Lower Three Gates (*xia san yin* 下三陰). The Lower Three Gates is a fancy name for where our *qi* has a tendency to leak out in the lower torso. To cultivate *qi* and do the alchemical work we need to seal up the body.

The Three Lower Yin Gates

Front Yin (*qianyin* 前陰): genitals. For women this gate has two openings, one *yin*, one *yang*. For men, we seal where the genitals meet the torso, contracting and expanding to do so.

Middle Yin (*zhongyin* 中陰): the perineum (*huiyin* 會陰; note: this is the *huiyin* area not the acu-point). Although it is not a physical opening, it is an energetic gate. The *huiyin* seals when sitting cross-legged, so there is no need at this point to consciously seal it with *xiaofu* breathing.

Back Yin (*houyin* 後陰): the anus. Pull up and release to seal, but do not fully release. Leave it slightly closed.

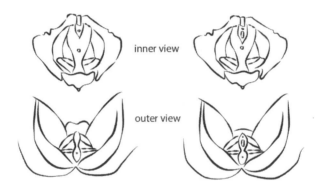

Huiyin Breathing

To seal the gates, start by simply contracting the area in question. The process is subtle. The seal is both physical and energetic, and sensing it takes practice and sensitivity. To make things more difficult, each of the gates works a little differently. Initially, it might be difficult to understand what is going on down there. The guided instructions offer a starting point. To aid in sealing the gates, some practitioners find it helpful to sit on a rolled-up towel.

Guided Instructions

> Breathe in, pull up anus, contract genitals,
>   contract *xiaofu*
> Breathe out, *xiaofu* expand, genitals release
> Repeat a few times

8. Inner Breathing

Inner breathing (*neixing huxi* 內行呼吸) happens inside the body. Although air is still going in and out of the nose, we do not focus on it. We focus inside. We forget about nose breathing and natural breathing. For the complete inhale and exhale, our focus stays inside without coming out of the body. If we are aware of the air coming in and out of our body, we are not doing inner breathing. This way of breathing begins the process of shifting from normal breath (*fanxi* 凡息) to True Breath (*zhenxi* 真息).

Inner breathing moves from inside the physical body. We focus on a certain area inside our body to drive the inbreath and the outbreath. Although this may sound odd, it is not that much stranger than breathing with our abdomen. The abdomen does not technically breath either. But somehow when we coordinate the contraction and expansion of the belly with our inhale and exhale, it feels quite natural. The whole torso moves with the breath. Breathing is contraction and expansion. When we regulate our breathing, we coordinate the movement of the body with the breath. With inner breathing, we are simply using a specific place inside ourselves to do it.

The most basic form of inner breathing is called Inhale Past Navel, Exhale Not Past Heart. As the name suggests, when we breathe in, we simply follow the breath down the internal centreline of our body past the navel into the *xiaofu*. When we breathe out, we follow the breath up the internal centreline, but not past the level of our heart.

To start, we focus on nose breathing. This is called nose breathing leading inner breathing. After a short while, we forget about nose breathing and focus on the breath moving between the level of the heart and the *xiaofu* area. The actual air does not pass the lungs. As the diaphragm contracts to draw the inbreath, there is a sense of downward movement. Focus your *yinian* on this movement up and down along the internal centreline.

Inner Breathing can also be used with a variety of other locations inside the body, such as the *xiaofu* and body pores. After getting comfortable with breathing past the navel and not past the heart, try it in conjunction with Pore Breathing (basic technique number four) and Lower Abdominal (*Xiaofu*) Breathing (basic technique number seven). Start with nose breathing and then shift to inner breathing. This allows time to shift awareness from outside to inside the body. This process can also use different cavities, organs, and energy centres. We just focus on the area in question: breathe in, the area contracts, breathe out, the area expands.

Inner Breathing

Guided Instructions

Breathe in, breath passes navel
Breathe out, breath does not pass heart
Repeat this process 24 times

Practice Notes

- Avoid random thoughts and stay focused.
- When you breathe out, relax your body and allow it to sink down.
- Keep your focus inside the torso.
- Forget nose breathing.
- Do not move upper body and keep shoulders dropped.
- Breathe past navel but not as low down as the perineum (*huiyin* 會陰).
- Slow down the breath. 30mins for 24 breaths is standard, but this takes practice.
- Optional: start with normal breath then switch to reverse breathing.

9. Lower Field (*Xiatian*) Breathing

Now we are getting somewhere. Breathing with the *xiatian* approaches actual *neidan*. As the energetic space in the centre of the lower abdominal cavity, *xiatian* literally means lower field. Some lineages call this space the *dantian*, but again Dragon Gate *neidan* only considers it the *dantian* after there is an elixir in it. Until then, it is simply called the *xiatian*, which needs to be found and activated. Working with the Three Fields (*san tian* 三田) is central to the practice of Dragon Gate *neidan*, and *xiatian* breathing provides an ideal starting place.

First of all, we know that the *xiatian* is a spherical energetic space at the centre of the lower abdominal cavity. The *xiatian* does not correspond to the physical body because it does not exist within the physical realm. Regardless, physical markers can assist in locating it. Here are some rough coordinates:

> **Left to right:** in the middle.
>
> **Back to front:** in the middle and straight up
> from the genitals, just in front of the perineum
> (note: this can change).
>
> **Up and down:** one to two thumb widths below
> the level of the navel.
>
> **Size:** differs. It could be size of grape or the size of
> grapefruit; that is for you to discover.

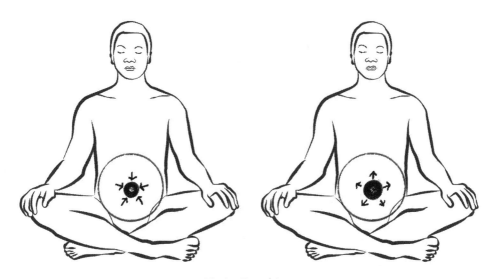

Xiatian Breathing

The *xiatian* is subtle. It takes time and practice to find and activate. It also requires stillness and focus. Even if you cannot find the space, you will still benefit from trying. Time spent pulling your *yinian* into your body is time well spent.

To breathe with the *xiatian*, you need to be comfortable with the other techniques in this chapter. You will not have much success with *xiatian* breathing if you are not able to do inner breathing or lower abdominal breathing. Start by putting your awareness into where you feel the space, even if it might later move. Then do some reverse inner breathing: breathe in, contracting the Lower Space inwards; breathe out, expanding the Lower Space outwards. To make it easier, start with *xiaofu* breathing and then after a few minutes shift to *xiatian* breathing. Once you have shifted completely, the outside of the body should not move. While breathing with the *xiatian* may be subtle, it eventually opens up with practice. Try to practice it every day for the best results.

Guided Instructions

First, take five to ten minutes to still your body and mind. To do this, start with some of the other techniques, such as body pore breathing, and then move to *xiaofu* breathing. After a few minutes, you will be ready to start the instructions below.

> Breathe in, *xiatian* gently contract
> Breathe out, *xiatian* gently expand
> Repeat this process 24 times
>
> Regulate breathing to be very even
> Slowly forget breathing and return to
>   normal breathing
>
> Stay focused on the *xiaofu/xiatian* area
> Look within, watch the changes of the
>   *xiaofu/xiatian* area
> Listen within, listen to the sounds of the
>   *xiaofu/xiatian* area
> Forget your breathing
> Forget your physical body
> Stay focused on the changes of the
>   *xiaofu/xiatian* area
> Do silent sitting

Working with the *xiatian* is key to *neidan* practice. The first Elixir forms in the *xiatian*. I have included *xiatian* breathing here in the Nine Basic Techniques merely as an introduction. There is no need to master it before moving on with the rest of the practices in this book. We will return to *xiatian* breathing in Chapter 11, The Lesser Reverted Elixir.

Those are the Nine Basic Techniques. Get comfortable with them. Play with them. Have fun with them. Always remember throughout the process that nothing is absolute. There are many ways to approach the training. Even these techniques, intended as an accessible introduction to Dragon Gate Taoist practice, form only a small part of the much larger collection of Yinxian Methods. While they may be used as a stand-alone practice, my hope is that they will provide you with a strong technical foundation for *neidan* training.

7

The Session

The basic skills you learned about in the last chapter are usually completed in a meditative state following a specific structure. I call this a session. This chapter will introduce the structure of a session, teach the opening and closing for each session, and provide a sample session by using some of the nine basic techniques.

Anatomy of a *Neidan* Session

A session captures each time we cross our legs, close our eyes, and do something (or nothing). It can last for a few minutes, a few hours, or even a few days. The session ends when we open our eyes and uncross our legs. For the beginning student, each session follows a basic five-part structure.

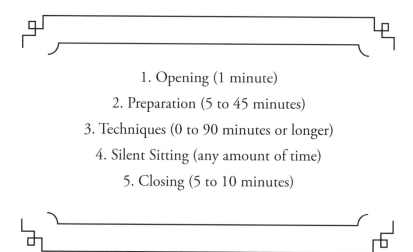

1. Opening (1 minute)

2. Preparation (5 to 45 minutes)

3. Techniques (0 to 90 minutes or longer)

4. Silent Sitting (any amount of time)

5. Closing (5 to 10 minutes)

Sitting for over two hours is best. However, work from where you are at. Increasing the length of our *neidan* sessions is the primary challenge of beginning students. Legs will hurt. Bodies will be sore. I could barely hold out for 20 minutes when I first started silent sitting.

The *neidan* process resembles the act of cooking. In Part 1, the Opening, you go into the kitchen. In Part 2, the Preparation, you bring out the necessary ingredients. In Part 3, the Techniques, you follow the recipe to turn on the stove, set up the pot, gather, prepare, and deposit the ingredients into the pot, put on the lid, and turn up the fire. In Part 4, Sitting Silently, you let the food cook. In Part 5, the Closing, you turn off the heat.

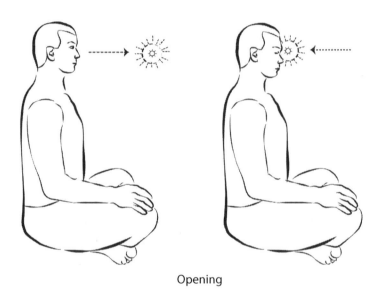

Opening

Part 1: Opening

The opening starts off the session, preparing us for the work ahead. It is short, lasting only a minute, but deep and multifaceted. In the past, students would often work on it for a year or two. But for now, let's just keep it simple. The exercise involves projecting our *yinian* outside our body in a horizontal line in front of our eyes as far as we can go. Check to see if we see any light. Next, slowly bring the *shenguang* (light of our spirit) back between our eyebrows in the same horizontal line. Whether we see the light or not does not matter. All that matters is that our *yinian* has come back.

The *shenguang* is a special light that we will begin to see once our practice deepens (see more in the next volume). We do this at the beginning of every session. Among other things, this skill allows practitioners to clearly and intentionally focus the *yinian* on the body.

Guided Instructions

> Get into position
> Palms down on knees
> Relax whole body
> Head up
> With eyes open, look to the horizon—the farther
>   the better
> Now your *yinian* is in the distance
> Slowly bring the *shenguang* back
> Back to between the eyebrows
> Gently close eyes

After the eyes are closed the session starts. The eyes remain closed for the entire session. After the opening we regulate body and mind to enter stillness.

Part 2: Preparation

Part 2 aims to prepare the self for the work ahead. We apply various Yinxian Methods to still the mind and body and return our *shen*. There are many techniques we can use, and many different sequences of techniques we can follow. My advice is to start with a couple of the Nine Basic Techniques presented in Chapter 6 and include pore breathing.

A good sequence for beginning students is to start with Inner Seeing (body scan), then move onto natural breathing, and then pore breathing with some body squeezes. This whole sequence might take 15 or 20 minutes. Feel free to experiment with the time and sequence.

Part 3: Techniques

This part works on specific techniques to get things done. Part 3 can have one or many steps, depending on the aim of each session. Think of each step like a building block. Once we understand the process of each block, we can move them around and change the order as needed. Specific techniques will be presented in the following chapters.

Part 4: Silent Sitting

Silent Sitting is where the magic happens. This part is about sitting in stillness. We forget our breathing, the physical body, and time and space. We just are. This is called entering a state of *wuwei*. We allow whatever we have done in Part 3 to bear fruit. Wang Liping recommends sitting silently for at least as long as the first three parts of the session, and it is preferable to double this time. Here are the guided instructions to take us into stillness. Follow these instructions once you have finished with the intentional *youwei* phase of your session.

Guided Instructions

> Look within, look at the changes inside the body
> Listen within, listen to sounds of the human universe
> Slowly forget your breathing
> Slowly forget your physical body
> Keep your *yinian* and *shen* inside the body
> Relax whole body
> Forget your breathing
> Forget your physical body
> Start silent sitting (sit for any length of time)

Part 5: Closing (Disperse Fire Breathing)

This part balances everything out, assuring that the body and mind return to a relaxed and stable state, and our *jing* and *qi* are balanced and smooth.

Each session also has a closing, which lasts between 5 and 10 minutes. Once you get the hang of *neidan*, each session can be quite eventful—the body changes, *qi* moves, and many other experiences can occur. Closing ensures balance, leaving the mind and body relaxed, stable, and still while our *jing* and *qi* are smoothly redistributed throughout the body. There are a number of different closing techniques. The most common is Disperse Fire Breathing (*sanhuo huxi* 散火呼吸).

Guided Instructions

> Slowly bring *shen* back to your body
> Slowly bring *shen* back to your body
> Relax whole body
> Relax both shoulders, arms, elbows, wrists, hands
> Spine Straight
> Lips gently closed, teeth lightly touching,
>   tongue touching upper palette
> Chin gently tucked in
> Regulate your breathing

Breathe light, even, and long
Inhale and exhale evenly

While regulating breathing, think about your
head, chest, abdomen and four limbs
Think about your external form
Now we do Disperse Fire Breathing
Follow the instructions

Breathe in, *qi* from all directions compress into
whole body pores
Breathe out, *qi* from body pores release into
surroundings

Breathe in, body pores contract
Breathe out, body pores expand
(Repeat 8x)

Breathe in, whole body contract
Breathe out, whole body expand
(Repeat 2x)

Breathe in, whole body contracts smaller and
smaller
Breathe out, whole body relaxes, body sinks down
(Repeat 2x)

Breathe in, body pores contract
Breathe out, body pores expand
(Repeat 4x)

Slowly return to natural breathing
Slowly let your body and heart-mind stabilize

Rub hands and face
Finish off practice

Example Session Using the Nine Basic Techniques

The following is a complete sample session that integrates some of the techniques from the last chapter. The session also acts as a template for methods later in the book. Just insert the various techniques in Part 3.

Part 1: Opening

Get into position
Palms down on knees
Relax whole body
Head up
With eyes open, look to the horizon—
    the farther the better
Now your *yinian* is in the distance
Slowly bring back the *shenguang*
To between the eyebrows
Gently close your eyes

Part 2: Preparation

Relax the whole body
Relax both shoulders, arms, elbows, wrists, hands
Spine straight
Lips gently closed, teeth lightly touching,
    tongue touching upper palette
Chin gently tucked in

Look within, look at your head, chest, abdomen,
    and four limbs
Look at the outer form of your physical body
Bring your *shen* back to your body

Natural Breathing

Regulate your breathing
Breathe light, even, and long
Inhale and exhale evenly
Breathe naturally now
Breathe without intention

But breathe light, even, and long
Slow down your breathing
So that your body slowly relaxes
So that your body is at ease
Regulate natural breathing
Breathe light, even, and long

As you regulate natural breathing, look within
Look at your head, chest, abdomen, and
    four limbs
Look at the outer form of your physical body
Bring your *shen* back to your body

Nose Breathing

Focus *Yinian* on your nose
Regulate nose breathing
Breathe light, gentle, and long
Inhale and exhale evenly
Look within, look at your nose
Regulate nose breathing
The nose is the centre point of the head
As you regulate nose breathing, think of your
    eyes, nose, mouth, ears
The seven upper openings
Check that these seven openings are
    properly sealed
Eyes must not look out
Ears must not listen out
Nose must not smell
Mouth must be closed
All seven openings are sealed

Body Pore Breathing

Now you are regulating gentle nose breathing
Use gentle nose breathing to activate body pores
Let body pores move with gentle nose breathing
Body pores contract, breathe in
Body pores release, breathe out

Breathe in, contract body pores
Breathe out, release body pores
Let body pores move with gentle nose breathing
Now you are using nose breathing to move body pores
Let body pores breathe with gentle nose breathing

Inner Breathing

Slowly forget nose breathing
Use inner breathing to move body pores
Let body pores breathe with inner breathing
Body pores contract, breathe in
Body pores release, breathe out
Now you are breathing with body pores
Activate whole body pores

As you regulate body pore breathing
Look within, look at your head, chest, abdomen
    and four limbs
Look at the shape of the physical body
Check whether the physical body is stable
Slowly bring your *shen* back into your body

Regulate body pore breathing
Check whether body pores are moving and breathing
If body pores are not moving, use gentle nose breathing
    to activate body pores
Use nose breathing to guide inner breathing
Use inner breathing to activate body pore breathing
Shift from natural breathing to inner breathing
Use inner breathing to move body pore breathing
Slowly return to natural breathing

The body is empty, empty but not empty
Shen is in the body, *shen* is in our heart

Part 3: Techniques

(*This sample session only contains preparation. If you want to go beyond preparation, this is the time and place in the sequence.*)

Part 4: Silent Sitting

Look within, look at the changes inside the body
Listen within, listen to sounds of the human
    universe
Slowly forget your breathing
Slowly forget your physical body
Keep your *yinian* and *shen* inside the body
Relax whole body
Forget your breathing
Forget your physical body
Start silent sitting (sit for any length of time)

Part 5: Closing

Slowly bring *shen* back to your body
Slowly bring *shen* back to your body
Relax your whole body
Relax both shoulders, arms, elbows, wrists, hands
Spine Straight
Lips gently closed, teeth lightly touching, tongue
    touching upper palette
Chin gently tucked in
Regulate your breathing
Breathe light, even, and long
Inhale and exhale evenly
Slowly bring *shen* back to your body
When regulating breathing, think about your
    head, chest, abdomen and four limbs
Think about your external form

Now we do Disperse Fire Breathing
Follow the instructions

Breathe in, *qi* from all directions compress into
    whole body pores
Breathe out, *qi* from body pores release into
    surroundings

Breathe in, body pores contract
Breathe out, body pores expand
(Repeat 8x)

Breathe in, whole body contract
Breathe out, whole body expand
(Repeat 2x)

Breathe in, whole body contracts smaller and smaller
Breathe out, whole body relaxes, body sinks down
(Repeat 2x)

Breathe in, body pores contract
Breathe out, body pores expand
(Repeat 4x)

Slowly return to natural breathing
Slowly let your body and heart stabilize

Rub hands and face
Finish off practice

8.

Furnace and Cauldron

To practice *neidan,* we first need to energetically seal the body and build up *jing* and *qi* inside ourselves. Without enough *qi*, not much can be done. In normal life, we spend much of our time focused outwards away from our body. The majority of the time, our senses are arrayed outwards. We watch, hear, smell, taste, feel, and think about the world around us. As we do so, our *qi* (in the form of *shishen*) leaks away. We rarely bother to look within ourselves, to turn around our observation and focus within our bodies, spend time listening to our heart, or get in touch with our kidneys. Taoist practice provides the opportunity to look within ourselves.

It is not enough to shift our observation. We also need to energetically seal the physical body. The body has a number of openings and gates where *qi* leaks away. We need to close these openings. Sealing up the body is known as Repairing Leakage and represents the first stage in the alchemical process. The key method we use is called Stabilize Furnace (*anlu* 安爐). After the body is sealed, we also want to set up a space to hold the *qi* with which we work. This space is called the cauldron. The cauldron is set up inside the furnace. We call this process Set Up Cauldron (*she ding* 設鼎). Both of these methods often proceed one after the other, and together they are called Stabilize Furnace and Set Up Cauldron (*anlu she ding* 安爐設鼎).

The furnace and cauldron are metaphors that are borrowed from external alchemy (*waidan* 外丹), which can be interpreted as cooking or baking. For example, if we want to bake a cake, then we need to prepare the ingredients before baking them. First, we need to get the oven ready and a pan in which to bake the cake. The oven is the Furnace. The pan is the Cauldron. Later we will gather the ingredients and put them into the pan and bake it. This is internal alchemy.

In the first alchemical phase, refining *jing* into *qi*, the furnace is the body and the Cauldron is either the *xiaofu* cavity or the *xiatian*. The furnace basically provides heat and the Cauldron holds the *qi* that we want to refine. Just a quick note here to mention is that the purpose of the Furnace and Cauldron will shift depending on the alchemical stage. For now, consider the Furnace the physical body and the Cauldron the lower abdominal cavity or *xiatian*.

There are a number of ways and a variety of techniques we can use to stabilize the Furnace and set up the Cauldron. In this chapter, I have included one way of doing it. Below are some guided instructions for Stabilize Furnace and Set Up Cauldron. Once you feel comfortable with the Nine Basic Techniques in Chapter 6, move on to this phase.

The method in this chapter is fairly dynamic, therefore it is helpful to first prepare. First take 5 or 10 minutes to still the mind and body. Also, it is best once we finish the method to sit in stillness for a time, and then finish with the closing from Chapter 7. Do you remember from the beginning of Chapter 7 how *neidan* sessions are structured? There are five parts: opening, preparation, techniques, silent sitting, and closing. The method below is done in Part 3, Techniques. We can also combine it in a session with other methods and techniques presented later in the book.

There are other ways to Stabilize Furnace and Set Up Cauldron. We stabilize the Furnace anytime we seek to still the body and bring back our focus and *qi*. We do this often in the preparatory stage of a *neidan* session.

This chapter incudes a method used to prepare us for the alchemical work. It provides a helpful starting point for working with the later practices in this book. However, we do not need to do this full sequence every session. Often doing a shorter version is fine. I usually use this sequence when working with new students or beginning a workshop. How we apply these methods in our own practice can be confusing for a new student. Wang Liping recommends noticing how we feel after a technique and remembering that feeling. Within Taoist practice, feeling is knowledge. The more we accumulate this kind of embodied knowledge, the more we will understand the practice.

When I practice, I try to know what technique my body needs. When my body needs a little of the old Stabilize Furnace and Set Up Cauldron, it is usually because I have not practiced for a day or two (like after my son was born), or when I have done too many silent sitting sessions and my body (the furnace) has cooled. But it really is just a feeling. When learning a new technique, I recommend doing it a fair bit in the beginning to get a feel for it, and subsequently apply the technique as needed.

Furnace and Cauldron

Methods vs. Techniques

One of the secrets of Taoist practice is to understand the difference between methods (*fa* 法), techniques (*shu* 術), and principles (*li* 理). There is a saying that "within methods are techniques, and within techniques there are principles, and within principles there are methods." Methods are the overall goal of doing something (the process), techniques are what we do to achieve it, and principles are the rules that govern things. While the meaning of principles is fairly straightforward, the difference between methods and techniques is less so.

Think of methods as strategy and techniques as tactics. Stabilize Furnace is a method. Pore breathing is a technique that is used to achieve the method, however, there are other ways of stabilizing the furnace.

In the old days, the methods were kept secret. Taoists would often share techniques with the public, but methods were kept close to the chest.

Stabilize Furnace, Set Up Cauldron

Guided Instructions

Prepare to stabilize furnace and set up cauldron
Look within, look at your head, chest, abdomen, and
    four limbs
Look at the shape of your physical body
Slowly bring the *shen* back to body pores
We have 84,000 body pores, the edge of the human
    universe

Breathe in, *qi* from all directions compress into
    whole body pores
Breathe out, *qi* from body pores release into
    surroundings

Breathe in, body pores contract
Breathe out, body pores expand
(Repeat 2x)

Breathe in, contract whole body
Breathe out, whole body expand
(Repeat 2x)

Breathe in, body pores contract
Breathe out, body pores expand
(Repeat 8x)

Breathe in, contract whole body
Breathe out, whole body expand
(Repeat 2x)

Breathe in, body pores contract
Breathe out, body pores expand
(Repeat 8x)

Breathe in, gather *yinian* on our head pores
Breathe out, head pores expand

Breathe in, head pores contract
Breathe out, head pores expand
(Repeat 4x)

Breathe in, two ears contract
Breathe out, two ears expand
(Repeat 4x)

Breathe in, head pores contract
Breathe out, head pores expand
(Repeat 4x)

Breathe in, move *yinian* slowly down the inner
    centreline of the body
Breathe out, move *yinian* into the *xiaofu/xiatian* area

Breathe in, *xiaofu* contract
Breathe out, *xiaofu* expand
(Repeat 6x)

Breathe in, pull up anus, contract genitals, contract
    xiaofu
Breathe out, *xiaofu* expand, genitals expand
(Repeat 4x)

Breathe in, *xiaofu* slowly contract
Breathe out, *xiaofu* slowly expand
(Repeat 4x)

Breathe in, *qi* from all directions compress into
    whole body pores
Breathe out, *qi* from body pores release into
    surroundings

Breathe in, body pores contract
Breathe out, body pores expand
(Repeat 2x)

Breathe in, whole body contract
Breathe out, whole body expand
(Repeat 2x)

Breathe in, body pores contract
Breathe out, body pores expand
(Repeat 8x)

Breathe in, whole body contract
Breathe out, whole body expand
(Repeat 2x)

Breathe in, body pores contract
Breathe out, body pores expand
(Repeat 8x)

Breathe in, contract whole body
Breathe out, whole body expand
Breathe in, contract body tighter and tighter
Breathe out, relax body, body sinks down

Breathe in, whole body contract, contract *xiaofu*
Breathe out, *xiaofu* expand, whole body expand
(Repeat 2x)

Breathe in, *xiaofu* contract
Breathe out, *xiaofu* expand
(Repeat 6x)

Breathe in, *xiaofu* contracts, contract *xiatian*
Breathe out, *xiatian* expands, *xiaofu* expands
(Repeat 2x)

Breathe in, *xiatian* contracts
Breathe out, *xiatian* expands
(Repeat 12x)

Slowly return to natural breathing
Relax whole body
Look within, watch the changes inside the body
Listen within, listen to sounds of the human universe

Stabilize Furnace and Set Up Cauldron is a central part of the alchemical process. It also contains a number of real-world applications. First off, the practice helps us to get into the body. After a busy day, our *shen* becomes scattered all over the place. We call this *shen chu* 神出, or the *shen* has left the body. This is the opposite of *chu shen* 出神, where our *shen* consciously and actively exits the body. The practice used in this chapter presents a powerful way of bringing the *shen* back into our body, and thereby also drawing ourselves back into the body.

The practice also assists with activating our inner *qi* (*neiqi* 內炁). Stabilizing the furnace and setting up the cauldron already starts changing *jing* into *qi*. The *qi* that is refined is different than *qi* used in many other internal arts such as qigong and tai chi (more on this in future volumes). *Jing* can be changed into *qi* anywhere in the body. We simple focus on and work the body in the correct way to begin the process, which is what Stabilize Furnace and Set Up Cauldron achieves. Not only does the practice get us into our body, sealing it up, it also begins building up our Inner Qi.

The Stabilize Furnace sequence included here relies heavily on pore breathing, which has wide-ranging benefits even beyond this sequence. Pore breathing cleans us out. When we breathe in, we draw Pre-heaven Original *Qi* into our bodies from our environment. We also expel turbid *qi* from inside the body to outside. Turbid *qi* is often characterized as old, stagnant, or blocked *qi* that can cause illness (see boxed text on page 17: *Turbid Qi*). This process is essential for health and well-being. It is an ongoing natural process that we are simply learning to augment. When old stagnant *qi* builds up inside the body, illness sets in. From the Taoist perspective, movement equals health and stagnation results in sickness. Pore breathing keeps things moving, both inside the body and between inside and outside. Especially when we throw in the body squeeze, but more on that below.

Although from the perspective of our *shishen*, we are sealing up the body. Pore breathing can also create a more energetically porous and connected body. Part of the Taoist path is learning to experience the world around us energetically—that is to say, through *qi* in all of its manifestations. This is easiest when in nature because there is so much *qi*. However, as the theory goes, everything is *qi*, and even in the midst of the city, we are embedded within various energy fields (*qichang* 氣場). Learning to tune into these fields, feeling how they interact with our own energy field, is fun and a big part of our job as Taoist practitioners. Pore breathing is one of the best places to start this process.

Harmonizing with the energy fields around us is important for health and well-being. From my experience, energy fields are not good or bad in-and-of-themselves and do not associate with particular value judgements. From the perspective of Taoist practice, being in harmony with an energy field is good, while being out of harmony with our immediate environment is bad because it disrupts health and well-being. To harmonize and resonate with an energy field, we have two choices: adjust our own energy field to match it or adjust the external energy field to match our own. Pore breathing provides a great place to start.

Although pore breathing cannot directly regulate an external energy field, it teaches us through experience how to sense and connect into the energy field. It is a starting point. When we get the exhale right while practicing pore breathing, we learn to expand our *qi* outwards into the space around us. But the actual mechanics of how to regulate energy fields will have to wait for a future volume.

The body squeeze is another technique used in stabilizing the furnace that also has other applications. The body squeeze is fantastic for health. Contracting and expanding the musculature of the body releases held tension. The key is to make the breathing circular and continuous, while at the same time fully relaxing and sinking on the exhale. Once we get the breathing just right, every part of the body will begin to move. The contraction and expansion will begin penetrating deeply into the body, especially inside the torso. Along with the inside of the torso, the neck and head is called the Inner Cavity (*neiqiang* 內腔). Even though the Inner Cavity appears more predominantly both in and beyond advanced alchemical practices, the body squeeze effectively introduces the inner cavity. As the inside of the torso begins to move, the internal organs will also be massaged. Organ *qi* stagnation is a major contributor to illness.

As we go about our hectic daily lives, the internal organs often squish together and *qi* flow shuts down. The organs will begin to move as the movement of the body squeeze penetrates deeper into the torso. Breathing in, the body contracts and the organs are gently pushed together; breathing out, the body expands creating space between the organs. Stuck *qi* moves. Organs are massaged. Even bones will be realigned. And, finally, the major benefit of the body squeeze happens: all the *jing* and *qi* inside the torso evenly distributes. We can even begin changing *jing* into *qi* through this practice.

Stabilize Furnace and Set Up Cauldron prepares us for the alchemical work. The practice also improves health and well-being, as well as introducing something called *minggong* 命功 training. *Minggong* training engages our body and life force. You may have noticed that many of the practices in this book train the body as well as the mind, and Stabilize Furnace and Set Up Cauldron is no different. Now that we have sealed up the body it is time to go inside of it. In the next chapter we will learn to move and change *qi* inside the body.

9.

Alchemical Ingredients: *Kan* and *Li*

The next stop on our journey is moving *yinian* and *qi* inside our body and working with *yin* and *yang qi*. *Neidan* is an internal practice; it is *neigong*. Once we have stabilized our body and mind and brought back our *shen* and *yinian*, we can begin working inside. Even if we cannot feel our inner *qi*, we can still work with *yinian*. Chapter 9 presents a way to bring our *yinian* into the body, and then move it up and down the internal centreline of the torso between the *zhongtian* 中田 (middle field or Middle Dantian) and *xiatian*. This practice also works with *yin* and *yang qi*, the first two of the internal alchemical ingredients (*neiyao* 內藥, literally means internal medicine). We call this work *kan* and *li* practice.

Neidan uses a variety of metaphors to help orient us to the task of forming the Elixir. *Kan* 坎 and *li* 離 are two of the eight trigrams found in the Classic of Changes (*Yijing* 易經). Each of the eight trigrams represents a specific dynamic of change of *yin* and *yang*. *Kan* represents water and *yang* held within *yin*. *Li* represents fire and *yin* held within *yang*. The theory and application of the Classic of Changes is a lifetime of study in its own right. For now, we will focus on the fact that *li* is fire and *kan* is water.

Two fundamental principles shape *li* and *kan*: fire rises, whereas water settles and pools. In the alchemical process, fire and water come together three times. The first time they come together, fire represents our mind and water represents our body. Normally our mind focuses upwards and outwards away from our body. Fire (our mind) rises and water (our body) settles and congeals. We call this fire above and water below. Fire is above and rising. Water is below and sinking. There is no interaction. To begin the alchemical reaction, we invert this. We want there to be interaction. We bring our mind in the form of *yinian* back into our body. But it is not enough to simply bring it inside the body because we also need to sink the *yinian* down deep inside the torso, into the *xiaofu* area below the kidneys.

In Taoist tradition, the mind is connected to the heart and associated with fire. The heart is the seat of our mental activity, while the kidneys are the foundation of the physical body. The kidneys regulate our *jing* energy, and the *jing* supports our physical body. Heart is fire. Kidneys are water. We put fire under water. Once we have fire under water, we have interaction and basic building blocks of forming the Elixir. The fire heats up the water and creates something new: steam. This represents the first coming together of fire and water.

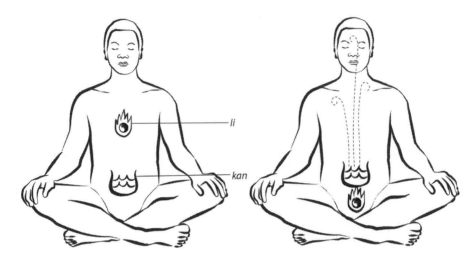

Kan and *Li*

Although we are using alchemical terms to frame our practice, we are not doing *neidan* quite yet. To do *neidan* we need a substance. We are not really doing *neidan* until we can feel and move our inner *qi* and *jing* energy. At this point in the process, we are still working with techniques from the Yinxian Methods, and not yet the Three Immortals Practice (*sanxian gong* 三仙功), which covers *neidan* proper.

The colloquial Chinese name for the breathing technique in this chapter is: inhale past navel, exhale not past heart. I call it basic *kan* and *li* breathing. This breathing technique uses inner breathing (see page 69, basic technique number eight: *Inner Breathing*).

We inhale following the breath inside the torso down the internal centreline of the body past the navel; we exhale following the breath up the internal centreline but not following it past the level of the heart. As with inner breathing, air still goes in and out of the nose filling the lungs while our focus remains inside the body.

Basic *kan* and *li* breathing is taught in three levels. At the core of this technique are the instructions: inhale past navel, exhale not past heart.

Level One

Breathe in, *yinian* and *qi* descend down the internal centreline of the body past the level of the navel

Breathe out, *yinian* and *qi* do not pass the level of the heart

Use hand movements

Level Two

The *yinian* and *qi* move between the *zhongtian* and *xiatian*

No hand movements

Level Three

Combines contraction and expansion of the *xiaofu* with the breathing of Level Two

Overview of Basic *Kan* and *Li* Breathing

1. Regulate gentle nose breathing to be very even
2. Optional: seal the seven upper openings (see page 56, basic technique number three: *Nose Breathing*)
3. Increase strength of breathing (not speed though)
4. Nose breathing leads inner breathing (attach *yinian* to breath)
5. Inner breathing has a path: inhale past navel, exhale not past heart
6. Forget nose breathing, just use inner breathing

Basic skills used

Nose breathing — Inner breathing — *Xiaofu* breathing (for Level Three)

Practice Notes

- Tilt head down slightly to help focus inside the torso
- If you cannot feel the inner *qi*, just work with *yinian*
- Use eyes to direct movement (Inner Seeing)
- Use ears to direct movement (Inner Hearing)
- Find the spine and stay in front
- Use other physical markers to stay oriented inside the torso
- Relax body, body sinks down
- Be very still
- No random thoughts, stay focused

The key to success with basic *kan* and *li* breathing is the setup. We start with nose breathing, and then move from nose breathing to inner breathing. If our nose breathing is not properly set up, then it is hard to get our *yinian* into our torso. Step Four of the *Overview of Basic Kan and Li Breathing* (see page 95) incorporates a technique to get into your body, which I call attach "*yinian* to breath". During Step Four, we follow the air into the nasal cavity through the mouth cavity, into the throat, and finally down to the inner torso. We focus on the air as it passes inside. *Yinian* likes to attach itself to an object. The breath becomes the object. As air is sucked inside, our *yinian* piggybacks along for the ride. Once our *yinian* is inside, we forget the air going in and out of the nose and just focus inside ourselves (Step Five). We can attach our *shen* to the breath once we are more comfortable working it.

All three levels rely on combining our *yinian* with our breathing. Once inside, the *yinian* travels up and down the internal centreline of the body along with the breath. The internal centreline is the vertical line that runs inside the body from the top of the head to the base of the pelvis. At this point in our practice, try not to consider the centreline an energy channel or meridian, although we can move *qi* along it. For now, try to use the line as a spatial reference inside the body. Getting our *yinian* inside our torso is the first hurdle. We try not to get lost in the process. The centreline helps our internal navigation.

Because the centreline is not a physical thing, the *yinian* still might need a little help to stay oriented. Here are some more coordinates. Left to right is fairly straightforward; front to back is where it gets tricky. When most people start, they will be at the front of the torso, or even outside their body. A helpful hint is to use the spine to orient us inside of the torso. Find the spine and stay in front of it. Also, use the perineum, which is called the *huiyin* area in Taoist practice. The centre of this area is the *huiyin* acupoint. The *huiyin* area is between the anus and genitals. The easiest way to find the *huiyin* is to pull up on it slightly. The centreline ascends from the front part of the *huiyin* area, close to the genitals. (Note: the internal centreline is not the thrusting meridian at this point in our training.)

Again, we will work with guided instructions to do the practice. The instructions are fairly structured, which helps hardwire the practice in the body. After we have embodied the method, try to play with it by changing the number of breaths or shifting the focus area. Just remember that it is best to use the basic *kan* and *li* breathing technique in a *neidan* session, starting with opening and preparation, and followed by silent sitting and closing. We also might wish to combine it with other techniques such as Stabilize Furnace and Set Up Cauldron. But that is up to you. Refer to the beginning of Chapter 7 for how to use the guided instructions.

Yin and *Yang*

There is night because there is day, soft because there is hard, up because there is down. *Yin* and *yang* presents a conceptual model used to make sense of the world around us. The ancient Chinese saw the world around them as existing because of opposites. These opposites seemed to follow a certain pattern and were called *yin* and *yang*. The words *yin* and *yang* originally referred to the shady and not shady side of a hill. The shady side of the hill was called *yin* and the side that was bathed in sunlight was known as *yang*. By extension, *yang* came to mean what is active, bright, and hot, while *yin* is passive, dark, and cool. Regardless of these oppositional states, it is important to bear in mind that *yin* and *yang* only mean something in relation to each other. A thing is not inherently *yin* and *yang*; it only becomes *yin* and *yang* when compared with something else. Put another way, it is theory that we apply to data.

Level One

Start with Level One and move on to Level Two and Three as you get comfortable with the techniques or if you get bored. Level One includes hand movements. The hands help coordinate and guide the *yinian* and *qi* inside of the body. This is called using the external to lead the internal. Until our *shen* is strong and clear, we use our hands to help lead the *qi*.

Hand Movements

1. Start with hands in front of chest at level of nipples palms facing down, with fingertips of each hand facing each other. Relax shoulders, arms, elbows, wrists, and hands.

2. As we breathe in, hands move down, leading the movement inside. Palms face downwards.

3. Go well past navel until palms are almost in your lap, then turn palms upwards.

4. Breathe out, moving hands up and leading movement inside. Palms face upwards.

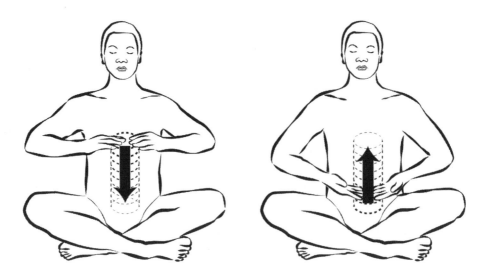

Kan and *Li* hand movement

Guided Instructions (Level One)

Regulate gentle nose breathing
Breathe light, gentle, and long
Inhale and exhale evenly
Slow down your breathing

Regulate breathing to be very even
Slowly increase the strength of your breathing
Breathe fine, deep, and long
Inhale and exhale evenly

Use nose breathing to guide inner breathing
Shift from normal breathing to inner breathing
This time our inner breathing has a path:
Breathe in, *qi* past navel, breathe out, *qi* not past heart
Forget nose breathing

Inhale past navel
Exhale not past heart
(Repeat 24x)

Last breath, breathe in past navel, stay in *xiaofu* cavity
Breathe out, relax body, stay focused in *xiaofu* cavity

Return to natural breathing

Level Two

Level Two is the same as Level One but with a sharper focus. The route is the same but instead of simply moving our *yinian* between the chest and lower abdominal cavities, we move it between the *zhongtian* and *xiatian*. The Three Fields are important spaces in *neidan* practice. The middle field is in the centre of the chest cavity, on the same level as our nipples (right next to the heart). The *xiatian* is in the centre of the *xiaofu* cavity. We found it when learning *xiatian* breathing (see page 71, basic technique number nine: *Lower Field (Xiatian) Breathing*). At this point it does not matter whether you can feel your fields or not. For now, the key is getting your *yinian* into the general area. Hands are not required for Levels Two and Three.

Kan and *Li* with *Xiatian* and *Zhongtian*

Guided Instructions (Level Two)

Slowly regulate gentle nose breathing
Breathe fine, gentle, and long
Inhale and exhale evenly
Slow down your breathing

Regulate breathing so that it is very even
Slowly increase the strength of your breathing
Breathe fine, deep, and long
Inhale and exhale evenly

Use nose breathing to guide inner breathing
Shift from normal breathing to inner breathing
This time your inner breathing has a path:
Breathe in, *qi* passes navel, breathe out, *qi* not past heart

Breathe in, *qi* passes navel
Breathe out, *qi* not past heart
(Repeat 3x)

Breathe in, *qi* passes navel to *xiatian*
Breathe out, *qi* not past heart, arrive at *zhongtian*
(Repeat 3x)

Breathe in, *yinian* at *xiatian*
Breathe out, *yinian* at *zhongtian*

Breathe in, use Inner Seeing to look at *xiatian*
Breathe out, use Inner Seeing to look at *zhongtian*

Breathe in, *qi* passes navel to *xiatian*
Breathe out, *qi* not past heart, arrive at *zhongtian*
(Repeat 4x)

Breathe in, *yinian* at *xiatian*
Breathe out, *yinian* at *zhongtian*

Breathe in, use Inner Seeing to look at *xiatian*
Breathe out, use Inner Seeing to look at *zhongtian*

Breathe in, *qi* passes navel to *xiatian*
Breathe out, *qi* not past heart, arrive at *zhongtian*
(Repeat 4x)

Last breath, breathe in, *qi* passes navel, stay in *xiatian*
Breathe out, relax body, stay focused on *xiatian*

Return to natural breathing

Level Three

Now we will add lower abdominal (*xiaofu*) breathing into the mix. In Level One, we started with moving our *yinian* and *qi* up and down the internal centreline of the body between the chest cavity and the lower abdomen with our hands. Then we focused on moving our *yinian* and *qi* between the *zhongtian* and *xiatian* as we breathed in and out. In Level Three, we contract and expand the *xiaofu* with our breathing. We still breathe in past the navel to the *xiatian*, but we also contract the *xiaofu* as we do it. This requires some coordination to get right. The *xiaofu* begins contracting with the inhale and the *yinian* already moving. As a quick pointer, it can also help to move the *yinian* right to the next destination as soon as we start the next breath. *Yi* is very fast. There is an old saying that *yi* arrives first and then *qi* follows, an aspect of the practice that will be explored more in the next chapter. At this stage, try to just play around with the timing of the various components in this level.

The guided instructions for Level Three are more complex. It contains all the components put together in a nice dynamic package. Wang Liping often only teaches

Level Three to make most efficient use of his time with students. However, if you feel the instructions are a little too involved, then consider following the basic breathing, *yinian* movements, and *xiaofu* movements without the other instructions.

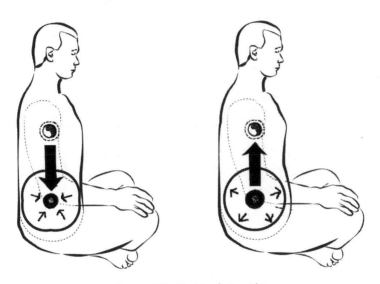

Kan and *Li* with *Xiaofu* Breathing

Guided Instructions (Level Three)

Slowly regulate gentle nose breathing
Breathe fine, gentle, and long
Inhale and exhale evenly
Slow down your breathing

Regulate breathing so that it is very even
Slowly increase the strength of your breathing
Breathe fine, deep, and long
Inhale and exhale evenly

Use nose breathing to guide inner breathing
Shift from normal breathing to inner breathing
This time your inner breathing has a path:
Breathe in, *qi* passes navel, breathe out, *qi* not past heart

Breathe in, *qi* passes navel
Breathe out, *qi* does not pass heart
(Repeat 3x)
Breathe in, *qi* passes navel, contract *xiaofu*
Breathe out, *qi* does not pass heart, *xiaofu* expands
(Repeat 3x)

Breathe in, *yinian* at *xiatian*
Breathe out, *yinian* at *zhongtian*

Breathe in, use Inner Seeing to look at *xiatian*
Breathe out, use Inner Seeing to look at *zhongtian*

Breathe in, *qi* passes navel to *xiatian*, contract *xiaofu*,
    yinian at *xiatian*
Breathe out, *qi* does not pass heart, *xiaofu* expand,
    yinian at *zhongtian*

Breathe in, *qi* passes navel to *xiatian*, contract *xiaofu*
Breathe out, *qi* does not pass heart, *xiaofu* expands
(Repeat 4x)

Breathe in, *qi* passes navel to *xiatian*, contract *xiaofu*,
    stop in *xiatian*
Breathe out, *xiaofu* expands, *yinian* stays in *xiatian*

Breathe in, *xiaofu* slowly contracts inwards
Breathe out, *xiaofu* slowly expands outwards
(Repeat 4x)

Breathe in, *xiaofu* contracts, contract *xiatian*
Breathe out, *xiatian* expands, expand *xiaofu*
(Repeat)
Breathe in, *xiatian* contracts
Breathe out, *xiatian* expands
(Repeat 8x)

Return to natural breathing

The basic *kan* and *li* breathing practice takes us deeper into our body and helps us learn to move around inside the torso. The practice also sets up our interior heaven and earth. The expression interior heaven and earth is often used in Taoist practice. There are actually two heaven and earths that we set up inside the body. When talking about heaven and earth, heaven (*tian* 天) simply means the sky or the heavens above, not the heaven beyond Saint Peter's Pearly Gate.

Dating back to ancient China, "heaven and earth" has referred to a metaphysical idea that a world comes into being by splitting into *yin* and *yang*. *Yin qi* descends, settles, and pools, becoming the earth. *Yang qi* rises and becomes the sky, or heaven. Heaven is *yang*, and earth is *yin*. The heavens above our head remain active and ever-changing. Weather comes and goes, and the heavenly bodies are in constant motion. The ancient Chinese see the sky as being in a dominant position to the earth. The earth receives whatever the sky unleashes. The earth is passive and relatively unchanging. Each world, or discreet domain, follows this dynamic. The inside of the body is no different.

Once we seal off the body, we set up our own personal domain. In order to properly set up our own universe, we need to establish an interior heaven and earth. This structures *yin* and *yang qi* inside and gives us a space to work within. We call this setting up a *taiji* 太極. We move from a *wuji* 無極 state, where there is no differentiation, to *taiji*, where there is difference and therefore perspective and relationship. *Wuji* literally means no poles. *Taiji* means extreme poles. Once *yin* and *yang* properly divide within a space, the taiji is set up, and the space becomes its own domain with perspective and relationship between things. We can set up a *taiji* in the body or even within a certain cavity or internal organ.

There are two interior heaven and earths. In the first one, the head is heaven and the lower abdominal cavity is earth. In the second one, the chest cavity or *zhongtian* is heaven and the lower abdominal cavity or *xiatian* is earth. Basic *kan* and *li* breathing sets up the second, smaller interior heaven and earth. Setting up the first one uses Stabilize Furnace and Set Up Cauldron, as we practiced in the last chapter. Working with heaven and earth inside the body establishes a foundation for working with *yin* and *yang qi*, which are both alchemical ingredients for the elixir. Now that we have put the two *qi* forms of *yin* and *yang* into the *xiatian*, it is time to start gathering the five-phase *qi* from the organs.

10.

Alchemical Ingredients: Five Phases

The physical body is the foundation of Taoist practice, and *neidan* is no different. For Taoists, the body is a sacred space, which explains why for a few millennia they have been exploring its inner landscape. In Chapter 10, we begin to probe our internal topography in more detail. Organs are a primary feature of the inner landscape, and using Five Phase Organ Practice to open the Maoyou Cosmic Orbit is a great way to start. However, the Five Phase Organ Practice is more than just a journey through the body; it is a core practice of Wang Liping's *neidan*.

The first stage of the alchemical work is refining *jing* into *qi*. To do this, we gather the *jing* energy inside our body and move it into the *xiatian* turning it into *qi*. *Jing* energy connects closely to our physical body. As far as energy goes, it is fairly dense. The majority of *jing* in our body is found in our internal organs and bone marrow. And the Five Phase Organ Practice (*wuxing zouxiang* 五行走向) serves as the best way, in my experience, to move *jing* into our *xiatian*. When we have refined the *jing* in our *xiatian* into *qi*, we have successfully completed the first elixir: the Lesser Reverted Elixir. Five Phase Organ Practice remains the key to achieve it.

Five Phase Organ Practice is the first of the Cosmic Orbits (*zhou tian* 周天) that we open in the Dragon Gate Lineage. Cosmic Orbits are circuits of energy we open in the body. The most famous in the West and amongst qigong practitioners in China is the Microcosmic Orbit (*xiao zhou tian* 小周天). However, there are a number of different cosmic orbits that open as we progress through our practice. In Wang Liping's lineage, the first orbit we open is called the Maoyou Cosmic Orbit (*maoyou zhoutian* 卯酉周天). The Maoyou Cosmic Orbit is an energy circuit through our internal organs and we use the Five Phase Organ Practice to get the job done.

Five Phase Organ Practice also serves as an effective method to activate our *xiatian*. At this point in our practice, the *xiatian* might be nothing more than a space. We might feel energy in our lower abdomen, but *qi* in the *xiaofu* is different than *qi* in our *xiatian*. To activate the *xiatian*, we need to put something in it. That something is *jing*.

Since much of our *jing* can be found in the internal organs, Five Phase Organ Practice is ideal for moving *jing* into the *xiatian*. Once we have *jing* in the *xiatian*, we will have something to feel. The *xiatian* is the battery for the meridian system, and once we get our *xiatian* going, we can work on opening the other meridians and energy channels in the body. In other words, the Five Phase Organ Practice is an important part of the *neidan* core curriculum, especially for the stage of refining *jing* into *qi*.

Even if we are not aspiring to immortal greatness, Five Phase Organ Practice substantially improves our health. The practice is a kind of *Minggong* 命功 and it nourishes and strengthens our physical body. After a session of Five Phase Organ Practice, I always feel fully in my body, ready to get on with the day. One of the most common experiences that my students describe when practicing the Five Phase Organ Practice is the amount of heat generated inside of the body. The organ practice also works to balance out energy in our organs, preventing potential formation of illnesses. The Taoists often consider the cause of illness as stemming from energetic anomalies in our internal organs. Five Phase Organ Practice works to prevent these anomalies before they emerge, thereby rebalancing the system.

Dragon Gate Organ Practice facilitates two main ways of working with organs: Single Organ Practice and the Five Phase Organ Practice. Although Five Phase Organ Practice is the most important method, we can also focus on one organ at a time. I will include methods for both. It is best to learn Five Phase Organ Practice first, but single organ practice presents another option, even though Wang Liping does not teach it very often. If you cannot get enough of working with the organs, then try out the Single Organ Practice as an additional option.

When we do Five Phase Organ Practice, we follow a circuit through the major organs in the body. The circuit we take is mapped out according to the creation cycle of the Five Phases (see boxed text on page 108: *Five Phases*). Internal organs in Chinese medical theory are separated into *yin* and *yang* organs. *Yin* organs are called zang. *Yang* organs are called *fu*. *Zang* and *fu* are paired together. Generally, *zang* are solid inside and include kidneys, liver, heart, spleen, lungs. *Fu* are hollow inside and include the bladder, gallbladder, small intestine, stomach, large intestine (note: we will not work with the pericardium and triple burner in this book). In our practice we will work with the zang. The only exception is the stomach and the bladder, which are both *fu*.

Following this cycle, we stop at each organ and work to transform the *qi* (*qihua* 氣化) inside it. The method we use when working with the organ changes depending on which level we are working on at the time. No matter which level, the circuit generally remains the same. We move the *qi* through a specific cycle. This cycle follows the creation cycle of the Five Phases (we can also reverse the cycle when working with Levels Two and Three of the Practice). Each organ system in our body connects to one of the Five Phases.

Here is the sequence:

1. Bladder (water)
2. Liver (wood)
3. Heart (fire)
4. Spleen/stomach (earth)
5. Lungs (metal)
6. Kidneys (water)
7. Bladder (water)

Organ cycle in body

We start the cycle in the *xiatian* and move down to the bladder returning to the *xiatian* from the bladder when we are done. In classical Chinese medicine, the bladder is a part of the kidney system, which belongs to the Water Phase.

The practices in this chapter fit into a *neidan* session in the same way as any other ones. We follow the structure laid out in Chapter 7. The practices in this chapter are techniques and fit into the third section of a session, right after the opening and preparation sections. The Five Phase Organ Practice begins and ends with *xiatian*. The best way to get into the *xiatian* is to use the basic *kan* and *li* breathing method explained in the previous chapter. As outlined, the breathing starts at the nose and ends in the *xiatian*, and from the *xiatian* we can jump straight into Five Phase Organ Practice. Even though Wang Liping often follows this sequence, there are also other possible orders to follow. Again, there are no absolute rules with Taoist practice.

Five Phases

The Five Phases (*wuxing* 五行, also translated as five elements or five agents) is another conceptual model used to understand our world. The Five Phases are not the same as the Four Elements (earth, air, fire, and water) here in the West. The name five elements came from a bad translation that eventually stuck. The Five Phases refer to five phases or dynamics of energetic expression. The phases include water, wood, fire, earth, and metal. These names are metaphors for the characteristic of the energy. As with *yin* and *yang*, the five phases only mean something when in relationship to each other.

Water: downwards (sinking and pooling)
Wood: expansion (outwards in all directions)
Fire: upwards (straight up)
Earth: circular and contained
Metal: contraction (inwards)

Five Phases

Five Phase Organ Practice

Three Levels of Practice

> 1st level—use outer force to move organ *qi* (hands)
>
> 2nd level—use inner force to move organ *qi* (no hands, *yinian* and *shen*)
>
> 3rd level—use cosmic force to move organ *qi* (*yinian* and *shenguang*)

Practice Notes

- Be gentle with your heart, use gentle *yinian* and breathing
- Practice can be done standing, but eyes need to be closed
- Complete cycle can be done multiple times (3 or 6 times work well)
- Keep the *qi* unified
- Coordinate *yinian*, eyes, hands, and *qi*
- When using Inner Seeing, look at organ instead of hands
- If working with one organ, and the next one in the sequence is activated, move to that organ right away. There is no need to finish the organ you are working on.
- Only the organ we are working with moves
- Stay focused—avoid random thoughts as much as possible

Level One

In Level One we use our hands to move and transform the *qi*, which is a process known as "using the outer to guide the inner." We use a variety of hand movements to work the organ with the goal of making a connection between the hands and the organ, while also using the hands to activate the *jing* in the organ to create movement. *Yunhua* 運化 is the Chinese verb for the process of using our hands to work with the organs. The meaning of *yunhua* comprises two words: move and transform. We use our hands to move and transform the *jing* energy of the organ. Another phrase used for the overall process of working with the organs is "move the *jing* to change into *qi*" (*yijing bianqi* 移精變炁). This old secret method first appeared around 2000 or more years ago in the Yellow Emperor's Internal Classic. The point here is to get the *jing* moving and transform it into *qi*.

Following the proper cycle, we work to activate and transform the *jing* energy of each organ. There are a number of ways we can use force with different types of hand movements. However, key to the practice is feeling the connection between the hands and the organ. First move the hands over the area of the organ, with the centre of the palms facing the organ. Leave about a centimeter or two of space between the hands and the body. The distance is determined by whether you can feel a connection between the palms and the organ. The connection will be subtle at first, perhaps just a slight tingle or aliveness if there is any initial feeling at all. Try to be patient because the requisite sensitivity takes time to develop. With practice, the experience will expand. Just continue to ask yourself as you practice: what do I feel?

Gaining any real traction with the organ practice requires directly feeling the organs. Figure out their size, shape, and location. I used to recommend that my students go online and do a little anatomical research into each organ. However, Wang Liping recently shared with us that when he started working with the internal organs, his teachers forbade him from looking at any anatomy textbooks or drawings. They wanted him to discover his internal landscape on his own. They gave him general location, but it was up to him to directly experience the organs for himself, free of as many conceptual filters as possible. Taoist practice is all about direct experience. So, try to feel them. They are a physical reality.

Next, we move the hands. Once we feel the connection between the organ and the hands, we use specific hand movements to work the organ *qi*. The hand movements follow a certain sequence. When working with hand movements, it is important for *qi* flow to relax and drop the shoulders, as well as relaxing the arms, wrists, hands and fingers. Here are the movements:

Rotate (*huadong* 划動)

Rotate the hands around the organ, palms continuing to face the organ. Start with a clockwise rotation, and then when you feel like it, switch to counterclockwise.

Squeeze (*niedong* 捏動)

Use the palms of the hands to make a slight squeezing motion over the organ. The distance between the two hands should be about a centimetre. To squeeze the hands, only move the knuckle joints; the fingers remain extended. By flexing the knuckle joint, you activate the *laogong* acu-point (*laogong xue* 勞工穴) in the centre of the palm. The *laogong* is good for emitting *qi*. Imagine your hands kneading the organ. Slowly squeeze and open the hand in coordination with your breath: inhale and squeeze, exhale and open. Try to energetically squeeze the organ with the movement of your hand and the *qi*.

Pull and Push (*ladong* 拉動)

The pull and push hand movement resembles the squeeze movement but with the added dimension of pulling the hands away from the body and pushing them back towards it again. The *qi* connection with the organ determines the distance of the pull. Losing a sense of connection with the organ indicates the distance is too far. The move coordinates with the breath: inhale as you pull away, exhale as you push towards.

For each organ we usually follow the sequence of rotate, squeeze, pull/push, rotate. Nothing is written in stone, so feel free to make changes. Each organ should not take more than a minute. When going too slow, the *qi* could disperse. When moving too quickly, the *qi* does not have time to gather. Try to find the right tempo.

Although we use the same general movements for each organ, there are some variations listed in the following notes:

Liver: Because of its size, make sure to work all of it. Move the hands around to cover the entire organ.

Heart: Be gentler because the heart is delicate.

Stomach/spleen: The movement changes from a rotating to a slight pushing movement from left to right, following the direction of food going through the stomach.

Lungs: Because of their particularly large size, the rotate movement changes to a big opening motion with the whole arms. At the top of the rotation, the elbows are on the same level as the shoulders and the hands are above the shoulders. The movement provides a full expansion and opening of the chest. Apply the kneading and pull/push movement each time in different areas, moving up and down the chest to affect all of the two lungs.

Kidneys: Hands move around to your back angling them upwards 45 degrees to properly face the kidneys. Make sure to relax the back and shoulders as much as possible.

The transition between organs is also important. When moving between them, we need to transport the *qi* from the last organ to the new organ. Use breathing and correct hand positions to aid the process. Breathe in as you move *qi* up in the body and breathe out when pushing *qi* down. Keep the breath long and smooth, the hand movements slow, and the *yinian* focused. Palms face upward to move *qi* up in the body. Palms face down to push *qi* downward. As we move the *qi* up, position the palms as if you were cupping the *qi*, carrying it to the next destination. Also, hold the palms fairly level.

Using the hands is another method of filling the organs with *qi*. The Laogong in our palms emits *qi*. By working the organs with the hands, the organs get charged up. We call this *zhuang yao* 裝藥 or loading up the alchemical ingredients. In the first stage of the alchemical process, the ingredients, also translated as medicine, equate to *jing* energy. The more *qi* we load into our organs, the more *jing* we have to work with.

Guided Instructions

Slowly raise both hands and rotate *xiatian*
Both hands are rotating *xiatian*
Now pull *xiatian*
When pull, breathe in
When press, breathe out
When pull, breathe in
When press, breathe out
When pull, breathe in
When press, breathe out
Okay, now rotate *xiatian*
Rotate *xiatian*

Now push *qi* to bladder
Breathe out, relax
Rotate bladder
Rotate bladder
Now, squeeze bladder
Squeeze bladder
Now, pull bladder
When pull, breathe in
When press, breathe out
When pull, breathe in
When press, breathe out
When pull, breathe in
When press, breathe out
Now rotate bladder
Rotate bladder

Repeat same instructions for each organ:
bladder – liver – heart – stomach/spleen – lungs – kidneys – bladder

Draw bladder *qi* up to *xiatian*

Breathe in, *xiaofu* contract

Breathe out, *xiaofu* expand, two hands at *xiatian*
  doing rotation

Rotate *xiatian*

Now pull on *xiatian*

When pull, breathe in

When press, breathe out

When pull, breathe in

When press, breathe out

When pull, breathe in

When press, breathe out

Rotate *xiatian*

Rotate *xiatian*

Now slowly separate both hands and place
  on knees palms down

Whole body relaxes

Now five phase *qi* is in the *xiatian*

Now organ *qi* is in the *xiatian*

Now return to natural breathing

(to finish off the Organ Practice, we can do *xiaofu* and *xiatian* breathing to activate the *jing*)

Level Two

The student would traditionally practice with their hands until they could see their internal organs. To see inside the body, we use a method called Turn Around Observation and Look Within (*fanguan neishi* 反觀內視). At a certain point in our training, we are able to see our organs. It is a process that often takes time and practice. Many students start with Level Two before they can see their organs. That was my experience, and also for some of my students as well. My suggestion is to use Level One until you can distinctly feel the organs. Or, if you feel bored using the hands and want to try something new, give Level Two a try.

Level Two organ practice is called Silently Run Five Phases (*moyun wuxing* 默運五行). In Level Two, we move the *qi* using our *yinian* and *shen*, not our hands.

We call this process *shen* leading the *qi*. Remember that *shen* is energy associated with our awareness. We use our intention to move the *qi*. In Level One, we used *qi* to lead the *shen*. As we moved our hands, the *qi* would lead the *shen* and *yinian*. Now we work the other way by leading with our intention. We focus on where we want to direct the *qi* and it will follow. This is called "*yi* arrives then *shen* arrives; *shen* arrives then *qi* arrives." This is a higher level of internal work.

The circuit we work through remains the same as Level One. Start at the *xiatian* and move to the bladder; from the bladder, complete the cycle and return to the *xiatian* from the bladder. By returning to the *xiatian*, we are depositing the alchemical ingredients (*jing*) from the organs into the cauldron (*ruyao* 入藥) and preparing it to change into *qi*—and maybe even an Elixir (see next chapter). We can also refine *jing* into *qi* in the organs, but we can only form the Elixir in one of the Three Fields.

In Level Two, we also coordinate our *yinian* with our breathing. Use the guided instructions from Level One, but substitute with the following additions when arriving at each organ.

Guided Instructions

> Breathe in, [insert name of organ] contract
> Breathe out, [insert name of organ] expand
> Repeat 4 times for each organ

When arriving at an organ, breathe in and contract the organ. When you breathe out, the organ expands. The outside of the body does not move. The organ contracts and expands. At first this might feel a little strange. How can an organ contract? In the beginning it is a very subtle energetic movement. If you cannot initially feel the movement, then just contract and expand your *yinian* on the organ. Even just getting your *yinian* onto the internal organs benefits your health and cultivates the practice of *neidan*. Throughout the process stay as focused as possible, avoiding any random thoughts.

As with Level One, keep the *qi* and *yinian* together when moving between organs. Breathe in going up, breathe out going down. Breathe long and carefully. Internal *qi* can be delicate. When moving the *qi* from the *xiatian* into the bladder, slowly pull up on the genitals (for men just contract where the 'equipment' attaches to the torso, not the genitals themselves). Doing this helps get the *qi* into the bladder and not leaked out of the body. The bladder is of special interest because we often mistake the bladder for the *xiatian*. It is a common mistake to think we are in the *xiatian* when we are actually in the bladder. Pulling up on the genitals can help orient us inside and move the *qi* into the right place. If you have trouble locating the bladder, try drinking two litres of water and sit quietly for a couple hours. You will quickly locate the bladder!

Once you feel comfortable with the above instructions, you can add another layer before moving to Level Three. Use the Turn Around Observation and Look Within method to look at the organ's shape, colour, and brightness. We can even stop breathing when first arriving at an organ to practice awareness of it. Stopping our breath creates a still point that we can use, but it is best done after an exhale.

Try to sense if the organ's *qi* transforms. We call this energy change (*qihua*)— or, the *jing* energy in the organ changes into *qi*. When an organ's *qi* transforms, there is sometimes a visual cue. If you see anything interesting, be sure to log it in your practice journal afterwards.

Level Three

Level Three is much like Level Two, except we use *shenguang* energy instead of just inner *qi*. Working with the Light of our Spirit is beyond the scope of Volume 1. I have included it for the sake of completeness. But if you have yet to learn Celestial Eye Practice, just ignore this for now. For Level Three, we start by working with the Celestial Eye. Once we see the light, we can bring it down into our *xiatian* and follow the same instructions as Level Two. A variation is to bring the *shenguang* all the way back to the Rear Celestial Mirror and drop it down each side of the spine to both kidneys. Then we can start to work the Five Phase Organ sequence from the kidneys for a full cycle ending with the bladder into the *xiatian*.

Single Organ Practice

The Five Phase Organ Practice is part of the Dragon Gate *neidan* core curriculum. I recommend practicing it often. However, the Five Phase Organ Practice is not the only method to work with our organs. We can also work with each organ individually. Single Organ Practices are supplemental. They are useful in certain situations, or if we feel like going deeper into one organ system. The Single Organ Practices include hand movement. We use our hands to guide our *yinian* and *qi* to purify and nourish the organ system. Five Phase Organ Practice also allows us to transform organ *jing* into *qi*. Unlike Five Phase, Single Organ Practices will only be effective when sitting.

Single Organ Practices are useful for beginning students wanting to tune into some of the major organ systems. When following both the nourishing and evacuation route of each organ, a practitioner will learn more about each organ than only through the Five Phase Organ Practice. Similar to the Five Phase Organ Practice in Level One, using our hands helps to concentrate and draw awareness to each organ.

People with organ illness will also benefit from Singe Organ Practices. Organ illness often results from a high concentration of *jing* energy in the organ. By focusing on a single organ, we can work to move energy blockages and redistribute the *jing*. Single Organ Practices are also designed to work with the evacuation route of the organ, which is helpful for cleaning it out and purifying the organ.

We can pick and choose which organ to work with, and we do not need to do them all. If you do more than two organs, then follow the Five Phase creation sequence above: bladder – liver – heart – stomach/spleen – lungs – kidneys – bladder. This will keep all the *qi* balanced and congenial. As a general rule, practice each organ twice, but you can also go three or six times as well. It is best to finish with a round of Five Phase Organ Practice to balance the organ system out.

Before getting started, here is a note about treating organs with specific health issues. Wang Liping's approach to medical applications of *neidan* techniques usually involves a less-is-more approach. While there a range of applications to heal organ disfunction, attempting to fix an issue without proper guidance often creates more problems. Organs all work together in a complex web of energetic relationships. The system works best when balanced. Do not focus too much attention on fixing one organ at the expense of the others. A problem with one organ is often caused by an issue with another organ. Although it may be useful to focus on one organ system at a time, it is best to address the whole system supported by the Five Phase Organ Practice. Taoist alchemy training often reminds us that we are not as smart as we think. Sometimes the best approach to health and wellbeing is to simply bring awareness to the system as a whole and allow the body's intelligence to do the rest.

Lungs

Long ago lungs were called the Golden Flower Tree. The roots were the thoracic spine, the trunk the bronchus, and the branches the finer air passageways in the lungs. Below are the steps to work with the lungs:

1. Cross hands in front of lower abdomen, palms up (either hand on top).

2. Inhale one deep breath, at the same time bring hands up in one outward arching movement in front of the face. As you inhale, follow the air from the nose into the mouth and down the throat. Attach your *yinian* and *shen* to the air as it goes downwards into your torso.

3. Palms facing down, pressed upon each other following the windpipe to where it splits into left and right.

4. Palms follow both left and right bronchial passages on each side.

5. Both palms face towards lungs.

6. With palms facing towards lungs, nourish, activate and transform lung *qi* using the Five Phase Organ Practice hand movements: Rotate, squeeze, and pull. As you work to activate and transform lung *qi*, also use Inner Seeing to see size, shape, and colour of lungs. (Notice if the lungs look like a Golden Flower Tree, or perhaps look like a white tiger).

7. Pay attention to what lungs feel like, store this feeling in your body memory.

8. Two closing methods:

   a. Put hands back on knees, lift head, look forward, and let *qi* gather in lungs. Relax body; body sinks down.

   b. Use hands to guide *qi* down to the two kidneys. Then move the *qi* from kidneys to bladder, from bladder to liver, from liver to gallbladder. At gallbladder, use rotate hand movement for a little bit and then move to the duodenum (beginning of small intestine right after the stomach, where bile from gallbladder enters small intestine). Use rotate hand movements through small intestine, to large intestine, to colon, and out anus. Good for releasing toxins. (See stomach/spleen and liver single organ practice for more detailed instructions.)

Kidneys

The bladder and kidneys were once classified together as the kidneys. To distinguish between each, they called kidneys "back kidneys" and bladder was just bladder.

1. Move hands so that palms face two kidneys.

2. With palms facing towards two kidneys, nourish, activate and transform kidney *qi* using the Five Phase Organ Practice hand movements: Rotate, squeeze, and pull. At the same time, use Inner Seeing to see the size, shape, and colour of kidneys.

3. Push two kidney *qi* through ureter to bladder.

4. Bring hands to front of body to activate and transform bladder *qi* using rotate, squeeze, and pull. At the same time, use Inner Seeing to see size, shape, and colour of bladder.

5. Bring bladder *qi* into *xiatian*. Work *xiatian* using rotate, squeeze, and pull.

6. Place hands back on knees. Raise head and look forward. Relax body; body sinks down.

There is an alternative starting point for the kidney practice. However, only use it if you have started learning the celestial eye practice. Start by bringing the head up, eyes closed look into distance, bring *shenguang* back, back to *xue, mu, tian*. Bring the *shenguang* down following the two sides of the spine to two kidneys. Return to Step One above.

Liver and Gallbladder

This practice is particularly good for passing gall stones. If the stone is too large, however, it will first need to be broken down.

1. Cross hands in front of liver area, palms facing liver.

2. With palms facing towards liver, nourish liver *qi*, activate and transform liver *qi* using the Five Phase Organ Practice hand movements: Rotate, squeeze, and pull. At the same time, use Inner Seeing to see the size, shape, and colour of liver.

3. Use hand movements to energetically squeeze gallbladder. To work the gallbladder, use the squeeze movement. At the same time, use Inner Seeing to visualize the size, shape, and colour of gallbladder. See if gallbladder has an opening or not.

4. Place hands back on knees. Raise head and look forward. Relax body; body sinks down.

Optional closing: using *yi* and *qi* together, squeeze gallbladder bile and follow it through bile duct to the duodenum. Use rotate hand movements through small intestine, to large intestine, to colon, and out anus. Good for releasing toxins.

Heart

The heart is a delicate organ. Use gentle *yinian* when working with it. When activating and transforming heart *qi*, use gentle, light, and slow movements.

1. Raise both hands and face palms towards heart area.

2. With palms facing towards heart, nourish heart *qi*, activate and transform heart *qi* using the Five Phase Organ Practice hand movements: Rotate, squeeze, and pull. At the same time, use Inner Seeing to see the size, shape, and colour of heart.

3. When heart feels slightly warm, use both hands to move *qi* from heart towards the internal centreline of body.

4. Follow the internal centreline of body upwards with both hands and then out through lungs.

5. After lungs, separate hands and spread arms. Imagine the blood in the arteries following the movement of the hands and heart outwards. Go through shoulders, to arms, to hands, flowing all the way to fingertips.

6. Two hands come back and cross over lungs.

7. Move back down to heart. At the same time, imagine moving the blood in the veins from the fingertips, to arms, to lungs, and back to heart.

8. Again, activate and transform heart: rotate, squeeze, and pull.

9. Once again leave heart. Two hands follow internal centreline of body down to *xiatian* area.

10. Separate hands, follow down both legs to your feet.

11. Imagine blood in our arteries following the movement of hands, flowing to the tips of your toes.

12. Two hands follow back from tips of toes, up legs, and back to the *xiatian* area.

13. Cross hands in front of *xiatian*, palms facing *xiatian*.

14. Hands follow up internal centreline of body to heart.

15. Place hands back on knees. Raise head and look forward. Relax body; body sinks down.

Stomach and Spleen

The stomach and spleen route is the most effective Single Organ Practice for overall health.

1. Cross hands in front of lower abdomen, palms up (either hand on top).

2. Inhale one deep breath and at the same time, bring hands up in one outward arching movement in front of open mouth.

3. With hands still crossed, palms facing down and inwards, press breath and *yinian* into mouth and down esophagus. Mouth closes. Then follow esophagus (swallow any saliva too) down and to the left to opening of stomach.

4. Enter the stomach.

5. With palms facing towards stomach, nourish, activate and transform stomach *qi* using the Five Phase Organ Practice hand movements: Rotate, squeeze, and pull. At the same time, use Inner Seeing to see the size, shape, and colour of stomach.

6. After a while, use hands to push *qi* to stomach exit.

7. Use both hands, with palms facing small intestine, swing back and forth down the front of abdomen.

8. Use both hands, with palms facing and following large intestine, move up the right side of abdomen, across the top of abdomen, down left side to bottom, and then move to bottom centre of abdomen.

9. Use both hands, with palms facing colon, move up the internal centreline a little and then out anus.

Over the years I have come to realize that the defining characteristic that sets Taoism apart from other traditions is the deep focus on the body. The physical body is the foundation of Taoist practice. Taoist knowledge is found in the body. The conceptual mind can get us started, but at some point we need to leave it behind. This is why I have largely avoided theory in this book and instead focused on how to practice. Years ago, I remember when a student asked my first Taoist teacher about Taoist philosophy. My teacher took the student aside and showed him how to do an intense physical exercise that involved a continuous deep squatting movement. My teacher than said, "do that for a few years and we will talk later." Instead of talking, he got the student working with his body.

Now as a teacher myself, I appreciate how that teacher handled the student's question. I often have students who want to know the 'real' stuff. They lament that I only talk about breathing and how to practice instead of discussing esoteric knowledge, such as the meaning of the *dao* or where immortals go. There is knowledge to find and explore, but for Taoists true knowledge does not exist in the conceptual mind. True knowledge arises through the body and direct experience. To gain access to this knowledge, our body and mind must be trained. To begin on the Taoist path, we must first start by working the body.

Organs are a useful way to begin our epistemological journey because they are central to the body. Internal organs fill the inside of our torso. They are a significant physical reality. If we take them out, for instance, there is not much left inside. Organs in Chinese and Taoist understanding are more than just their physiological function. Each internal organ has an energy field and is situated in a broader system that includes sense organs, emotions, phases, and colours, as well as a number of other correspondences.

Organ (*Zang*, yin)	Organ (*Fu*, yang)	Phase	Colour	Emotion	Sense Organ
Kidney	Bladder	Water	Blue/ Black	Fear	Ears
Liver	Gall Bladder	Wood	Green	Anger/ Frustration	Eyes
Heart	Small Intestine	Fire	Red	Excitement	Tongue
Spleen	Stomach	Earth	Yellow	Worry	Mouth
Lungs	Large Intestine	Metal	White	Sadness	Nose

Wang Liping encourages practitioners to use the internal organs as antennas to sense (*ganwu* 感悟) the world around us. When an organ becomes energetically activated, we can look at its correspondences and acquire information. For example, if we walk into a new place and the energetic pulse of our liver strongly activates, there might be something related to anger or frustration (the emotion of the liver) in that space. This could be in response to a person or the space. Every space has an energy field that holds information of past events. Our body can pick up on these energetic traces when our own energy field interacts with the space or a person. If we are sensitive enough, our organs will communicate with us to help diagnose the issue. When this occurs, pay attention to the energy field of each organ and notice what is happening.

Gaining access to this level of information requires sensitivity to the energy fields around us and in our body. We also need to trust the information that arises. Using the conceptual mind to question whether the information is true or not shuts down the process. Evaluation is an important tool, but try to wait until after the event. In the beginning, much of the information might be incorrect. This is normal. It takes some time to understand the process. *Is that my stomach/spleen telling me that I need to sell my house or just the pizza I ate last night?* Be patient. Honing this skill takes time and practice.

The energetic condition of our internal organs also directly impacts our state of mind and sense of well-being. For the Taoists, each organ associates with an emotion (see chart, previous page). The condition of an organ will affect how and what we feel. In other words, our emotional experience links to our organs, ultimately demonstrating whether they are balanced or not. When we work with the organs using the techniques in this chapter, we learn to energetically rebalance the organ system. Stuck *qi* in one organ will move to nourish another organ that is lacking *qi*. The organ system returns to homeostasis. When this happens, our emotions also return to a balanced, neutral state. We still feel emotions, but we are just less overwhelmed by them. And vice versa, when our organs are disturbed, we are much more prone to express anger when someone cuts us off in traffic or to worry when we see that our bank account is empty. Our emotions impact our organs, and our organs impact our emotional experience.

Internal organs are also associated with our sense organs, which are connected with desire. Our *shishen* (Spirit of Recognition) exits through the sense organs and communicates with the world around us. The *shishen* is the part of our spirit associated with the senses and physical body. Living through the senses with our *shishen* creates attachment and desire, which impacts our internal organs. By working with the organs, we can release the attachment by releasing stuck *qi*. Our wild nature (*ye xing*) becomes tame. Taoists use the term wild nature to describe when our senses rule over us. When we live through our *shishen* and the senses, we get taken farther away from our true nature and our *yuanshen* (original spirit). One of the goals of Taoist practice is to live through our *yuanshen* as much as possible. Working with the organs can help us move towards this goal. By reconnecting with and rebalancing our internal organs, we minimize our *shishen* and maximize our *yuanshen*. We reduce our attachments and desires. The conceptual mind is also considered a sense because it recognizes our thoughts. Attachments to thoughts and fundamentalist thinking causes so much damage. Reducing this damage not only changes our lives, but also the lives of people around us.

The Five Phase Organ Practice profoundly affects our health. Sickness often begins with too much *jing* in an internal organ. The *jing* builds up over time and begins to energetically congeal as sickness develops. Organ practice works with the *jing* of our organs. When we focus on, and breathe with the organ, we activate and transform the *jing* of that organ. The *jing* either transforms into *qi*, or it disperses more evenly in the physical body. *Jing* is good. It gives us vitality. Stagnant *jing* is the problem. Five Phase Organ Practice keeps us healthy by dispersing *jing* before it can build up and cause health issues.

For Taoists, health and spirituality cannot be separated. Sickness is what keeps us from knowing our True Self (*zhenwo* 真我). Taoists say that it is a great tragedy when people are out of touch with their internal organs. Learning to feel, hear, and see our organs is essential for our Taoist practice. It is also vital for health, well-being, self-knowledge, and even self-love. When we pay attention to our organs, we nourish them with *qi*. This *qi* is a form of love. We learn about who we are and how to love ourselves throughout this process. In our contemporary lives, we often think of finding our self as discovering whether we vote left or right or whether we are a hockey person or a golf person. We usually do not think of finding ourselves through feeling our kidneys or hearing our liver. For the Taoists, this is precisely what we are doing. The True Self is found in the body.

Taoist Perspective on Health

For the Taoists, there are two types of illness:

1. sickness of body (*shen bing* 身病)
2. sickness of mind (*xin bing* 心病)

Although these terms seem familiar, for the Taoist they take on special meaning. Sickness of body is illness that arises in the physical body. Sickness of mind is illness that arises in the mind. Both sickness of body and sickness of mind influence each other. If we have illness in the body that goes untreated, it eventually leads to sickness of mind, and vice versa.

Sickness of body harms the body, and can be treated through:

1. Medicine (*yao* 藥)
2. Medical technique (*yi* 醫, note: *yi* is different in Taoist medicine than in classical Chinese medicine)

Sickness of mind harms others, and can be treated through:

1. Medicine
2. Curing (*zhi* 治)

Both kinds of sickness originate from:

1. Reincarnation energy (karma) and ancestral inheritance (genetic)
2. Environment
3. Social conditions
4. Sickness of body also arises from not being natural

Now for the kicker, we are all sick. It is just a matter of degree. From the Taoist perspective, all of us experience sickness of body and mind. Taoist training is all about providing guidance and practices to help us heal ourselves.

For the Taoist, the scope of sickness is very broad. Sickness of mind comes from having a "Sense of Self" (*zijue* 自覺). Sense of Self basically means that we think we are right and others are wrong. We hold a subjective perspective. Unfortunately, subjectivity is almost always wrong because its only limited to one perspective. Even the information in this book is wrong on some level! It is not considered true (*zhen* 真) in the Taoist sense. The sicker our mind gets, the more we harm others. In Western terms, we might refer to this as our ego-self.

The True Person (*Zhenren* 真人) represents someone who transcends the self and therefore no longer has sickness of mind. They have healed themselves. In order to do that, we also need to heal our bodies because mind and body are related (if not two aspects of the same thing).

Taoist alchemy is a powerful tool to help us heal. Both forms of sickness are connected with stuff inside the body, old stuff that is hidden away, such as past trauma and karmic crud. During a *neidan* session, once we seal up the body, sometimes this energy can come out. If the energy comes out as emotion, then it is a manifestation of sickness of mind. When this happens, bring the energy down to the *xiatian* and burn it using the *neidan* methods (see future volumes).

On a side note, the modern Chinese word for illness (*jibing* 疾病) is made up of two classical Chinese words *ji* and *bing*. These two words both refer to illness. *Ji* is a sickness that comes from non-physical causes, like mental illness or influence of bad *qi*, whereas *bing* relates to physical illness. *Ji* is sickness of mind, and *bing* is sickness of body.

11.

The Lesser Reverted Elixir

Forming the Lesser Reverted Elixir is what we have been working towards in Volume 1. The previous practices outlined in this book were used to get us here. Forming the Lesser Reverted Elixir (*xiao huan dan* 小還丹), sometimes called the small pill (*xiao yao* 小藥), is the first major benchmark in the Taoist alchemical process. We have taken the *yin* and *yang qi* and the *jing* energy of our organs (some other *qi* will come along for the ride) and put it into our *xiatian,* ready to fire.

Before going on, I should make a disclaimer. Learning techniques to form the elixir from a book is one thing, and actually doing it is another. Chances are that without direct contact with a teacher, we will not be able to accomplish the work. I include the method in this chapter mostly for reference. Feel free to try it out. But keep in mind that getting results is much easier when we have a teacher actively guiding us through the process. The same is true for all of the methods in this book, but even more so for this chapter.

We form the Lesser Reverted Elixir in the *xiatian* (Lower Field, sometimes called Lower Dantian). The *xiatian* is the locus of the alchemical work for this stage. The practices in this chapter will focus on the *xiatian*. We have been working with the *xiatian* since the Nine Basic Techniques in Chapter 6, and the instructions in this chapter are not much different. Now we are going to try using the *xiatian* to turn *jing* into *qi*. Refining *jing* into *qi* is not a single technique. It is a process and a feeling. There are instructions in this chapter but mostly it is just a feeling we get when we properly coordinate our breathing and *yinian* and body to work the *jing*. *Jing* can change pretty much anywhere in the body, but there are only three places we can change it and form an elixir in the process: Lower, Middle, and Upper Fields. In Volume 1 we focus on the Lower Field—*xiatian*.

In Dragon Gate *neidan*, there are several different elixirs we can form. The Lesser Reverted Elixir is the first and most basic. Here are some others:

The Elixirs

    i   The Lesser Reverted Elixir (*xiao huan dan* 小還丹)

   ii   The Greater Reverted Elixir (*da huan dan* 大還丹)

 iii   The Seven-Returned Elixir (*qi fan dan* 七反丹)

 iv   The Nine-Revolved Elixir (*jiu zhuan dan* 九轉丹)

  v   The Golden Liquid Elixir (*jinye huan dan* 金液還丹)

 vi   The Jade Liquid Elixir (*yüye huan dan* 玉液還丹)

Lesser Reverted Elixir

The Elixir we form in this book is the Lesser Reverted Elixir because the ingredients are from the organs. The Five Phase Organ Practice is where the action occurs. We have worked and opened the Maoyou Cosmic Orbit. Now all we need to do is work the *jing* in our *xiatian* and turn it into *qi*. We breathe with the *xiatian*. We gently pressurize the area by coordinating our *yinian* with the contraction and expansion of our inner breathing. The outside of the body does not move. We simply bring everything to bear on this single area. Our *shen*, *qi*, and *yi* all must come together. Turning *jing* into *qi* is surprisingly easy. The hard part is finding the *jing*. Once we tune into the subtle movement of the *jing*, the rest of the formation process will naturally unfold. There are still actions to take. Once the *jing* activates, it becomes more a question of endurance to see if we can hold the process long enough to reach fruition.

The Lesser Reverted Elixir will be different for everyone. Usually it is some sort of bright pulsing sphere of energy. The exact feeling of the elixir is for each of us to discover on our own. Wang Liping recommends avoiding exact descriptions because it can influence other people trying to locate and experience it. Although feeling the *jing* in our *xiatian* can be subtle in the beginning, the feeling becomes increasingly distinct once we learn to tune into it more. Noticing the sensation in our lower abdomen only ramps up as we get the hang of turning *jing* into *qi*. By the time we have the first stages of an Elixir inside, there is no way of missing it. Then the *xiatian* becomes a bona fide *dantian*.

The process usually starts with movement. The *xiatian* will begin to move, vibrate, pulse, or hum as we start filling the space with *jing* energy. When I first heard the moving of my *xiatian* consistently, it hummed like a quickly revolving fan. I would lay on my bed late at night as my *xiatian* would spin in time with the whirling of the big industrial fans on the snowmakers outside (I was at a ski resort in Korea). Even the humming of my refrigerator at home began resonating with my *xiatian*. It felt really good. The movement of the *xiatian* is a regular movement and has a pattern. If the sound is unregulated and messy, it is just the movement of *qi* in our lower abdomen. This is a key point.

Qi in our lower abdomen is great for health and forms the basis of many other neigong and qigong practices, but it is not enough for *neidan*. In Dragon Gate alchemy, the lower abdomen is not the *xiatian*. To reach the *xiatian* we must be incredibly stable and still. Our body must be relaxed and empty. The movement of the *jing* energy of the *xiatian* follows a regular pattern. Keep going until you find it.

The next sensation when activating the *xiatian* is usually heat. The *xiatian* gets really warm, even to the point where the lower body will sweat for a period of time. After the heat, light appears next. The *xiatian* will brighten up, even to the point of illuminating the whole of the inner torso. We call this inner illumination (*nei zhao* 內照).

After brightening up, the Elixir begins to solidify. The *dantian* becomes solid (at least it feels that way). It feels like there is a weight in the middle of our lower abdominal cavity. This is finally the Elixir. It should be noted that Wang Liping recommends not fully solidifying the Elixir yet. Return it. Before it solidifies, revert the energy back into the body. Living in the world with a formed Elixir in our belly can be quite intense. In forming the Elixir, we become very sensitive and connected to the world around us. This connection can be overwhelming, especially when living in our fast-paced modern world. Only if we are living as a hermit on a distant mountain top, or at the end of our life as an older person, is it advisable to fully form and hang on to the Elixir. Forming and reverting the Elixir is already excellent for our overall health. Also, the changes to ourselves and our lives that we will have gone through to get to this point are already phenomenal.

The Elixir can be reverted intentionally or unintentionally. If the Elixir wants to move, let it do so. This is considered unintentional reversion. The energy of the *xiatian* has its own intelligence (*xinling* 心靈). Letting this energy do what it wants highly benefits us. The Elixir knows where it needs to go. It will generally follow three routes: Microcosmic Orbit, Maoyou Cosmic Orbit, or up and down the internal centreline of the body and in the Three Fields. The Elixir is super-charged *qi*, so allow it to heal, nourish and recharge the body.

The Elixir can also be reverted intentionally. To intentionally revert the Elixir, breathe with the *qi* in the *xiatian* to disperse it. Use *xiatian* inner breathing to contract and expand, but now emphasize the expansion. When you breathe in, still contract just a little bit, and then breathe out and expand the *qi* bigger and bigger. Expand the *xiatian* until it fills the whole body. Then let the *qi* settle down and stabilize as you enter stillness and sit for a while.

There is more than one way to work with the alchemical ingredients in the *xiatian* in order to form an Elixir (*jiedan* 結丹). The method for firing the Alchemical Ingredients to form the Elixir is generally called the Firing Process (*qihuo* 起火). The firing process I have included in Volume 1 is gentle and basic. We focus on the *xiatian* and coordinate our inner breathing and *yinian* for a short time. Then we wait and see what happens. There are other ways and I will share these in future volumes, including the dynamic and intense Nine Times Firing Process (*jiuci qihuo* 九次起火). For now, enjoy the method below.

I want to conclude with one final point. As mentioned above, the energy of the *xiatian* has its own intelligence. *Neidan* practice is a Pre-Heaven practice (*xiantian* 先天). Amongst other things, this means we are working with our original substances: Original Jing, Original Qi, and Original Shen. This kind of energy will naturally go where it needs to go. If we try to control the process, it will only shut down. When we work with the *xiatian*, we must allow it space to move and breathe. Our practice is a balancing act between effort and effortlessness, between *youwei* and *wuwei*. Silent sitting helps. Silent sitting provides the requisite space necessary for the *xiatian* to form. When following the instructions provided below, make sure to end with stillness. Stillness is where the magic happens.

As with the previous chapters, we follow the guided instructions. The instructions for forming the elixir are used in the same way as previous techniques. Below is a sample session for forming the elixir. However, nothing is written in stone. At this point in our training, we should have a decent embodied sense of the techniques in this book and how to use them.

Session Structure

1. Opening
2. Preparation
3. Stabilize Furnace and Set Up Cauldron (optional)
4. Basic *Kan* and *Li* Breathing
5. Five Phase Organ Practice
6. Form Lesser Reverted Elixir
7. Silent Sitting: Used to Bathe and Cleanse the elixir
8. Closing

Guided Instructions

(Begin after we have done Five Phase Organ Practice and are breathing with our *xiatian*)

Breathe in, *xiatian* contract
Breathe out, *xiatian* expand
(Repeat 4x)

Gently hold your breath
Do not breathe
Check whether *xiatian* is moving or breathing
Now do not breathe

Slowly return to gentle nose breathing
Use gentle nose breathing to lead *xiatian*
Breathe in, *xiatian* slightly contract
Breathe out, *xiatian* slightly expand
Let *xiatian* move with gentle nose breathing
Now you use nose breathing to regulate *xiatian* breathing

Slowly forget nose breathing
Shift to inner breathing
Use *xiatian* inner breathing to activate the *xiatian*
Xiatian breathing is in the *xiaofu* area, outside of body
    does not move
Forget nose breathing, nose breathing does not exist

Turn around observation and look within
Look at *xiatian*
Yinian is at *xiatian*
Use Inner Hearing to listen to the *xiatian*
We want '*yi* arrives, *shen* arrives; *shen* arrives; *qi* arrives'

Your *yinian* is regulating inner breathing
Xiatian inner breathing
This inner breathing is inside the *xiaofu* area
Outside of the *xiaofu* does not move
When breathe in, *xiatian* gently contracts
When breathe out, *xiatian* gently expands
Gently pressurize the *xiatian*

Everyone's *xiatian* breathing is different
If *xiatian* breathing is too strong, the *jing* will disperse
If *xiatian* breathing is too weak, the *qi* will not
    accumulate
Use inner breathing to regulate the *xiatian*
Use Inner Hearing to listen to the sound of the *xiatian*
If you do not hear it clearly, gently stop breathing
While not breathing, relax body; body sinks down
Once we hear the sound of our *xiatian*, again return to
    xiatian inner breathing
Don't let sound of inner breathing be louder than the
    pulsing sound of the *xiatian*

Use Inner Hearing to listen to the *xiatian* pulse
Let the *xiatian* area pulse
Let it warm up
Let it slowly brighten up
Listen the sound of the *xiatian*
Let the pulsing sound of the *xiatian* get bigger, let it
    reverberate through your whole body
Slowly let the *xiatian* area settle down and stabilize
Slowly let it settle down and stabilize
Slowly let the *jing* energy of the *xiatian* area settle down
    and stabilize
Return to unregulated natural breathing

Forming the Lesser Reverted Elixir takes time and practice. Succeeding with the first elixir usually requires sitting sessions of at least two to three hours without moving. While working on it, there are other methods we can do to vary the process. For example, we can also practice *neidan* standing, walking, and even lying. These are called supplemental practices (see the last section of this book for detailed instruction). If your legs are getting a little sore from sitting around all day, then try out some of the supplemental practices.

Tips and Tricks for *Xiatian* Activation

Here is a list of tips and tricks for activating the *xiatian*, which is where the alchemical action occurs. But how do we find the *xiatian* and get the darn thing working?

First of all, we need methods. But what if, after we apply the methods, nothing happens? Below is a list of additional stuff we can do to facilitate the process. This list is by no means complete; it primarily provides some insights that helped me.

- Properly locate the *xiatian*.
  - Use the coordinates found in Chapter 6. Play around with the location as well. The spot where you think it is might be incorrect. It is easy to get disoriented inside the body. Try using external references like the navel to stay oriented inside.

- Figure out the knack ourselves.
  - Activating the *xiatian* requires us to use a special feeling inside the body. It is up to us to figure out the feeling. Igniting the *xiatian* requires a combination of using the right kind of focus in the correct area and softly allowing it to warm up and start moving. Imagine blowing on the ember of a fire to get a flame.

- Use Lower Space.
  - o It is right in the middle of this spherical space. If you know how, then you can compress the Lower Space to find the location of the *xiatian* quite easily. Working with the Lower Space helps to activate the *xiatian* as well.

- Figure out size.
  - o It will be a different size for everyone. In the beginning, there might not be much going on there; it might just be a space.

- Use *yinian* and *shen* properly.
  - o Get *yinian* and *shen* into the location. This will take focus and might be tiring. Finding an anchor point inside for the *yinian* will help. But try not to use overly strong focus. Muscling ourselves inside will not work. Find a balance. Move your awareness around the inside of the lower abdomen until you feel something. The feeling can be quite subtle at first, maybe just a tugging or a slight tremor.

- Use Inner Seeing and Inner Hearing.
  - o Inner Seeing and Inner Hearing help to focus the *shen* and the *yinian* in the body. I first stumbled upon my *xiatian* playing around with Inner Hearing, but everyone is different.

- Replenish *jing* and *qi*.
  - o If your *jing* and *qi* are not full enough, then you will not find the *xiatian*. Keep playing with the building foundation practices in Chapter 6. Also, working on foundation practices in general can also help replenish these substances in the body. Internal martial arts, *daoyin*, and qigong are useful but not essential for this process. Again, everyone's experience is different.

- Practice late at night and early in the morning (between 11:00pm and 5:00am).
  - o For me 4:00-ish in the morning is a fantastic time for practicing *neidan*. In the early morning the world is still, and stillness is essential for finding the *xiatian*. Midnight, known as Zi Time (zishi 子時), is also great for practice.

- Fasting.
  - o I first heard my *xiatian* after not eating for a while. Take a couple days off from eating and you will find that the lower abdomen empties, making it much easier to work inside the body. It is also easier to tune into the subtle body after fasting for a bit. However, be aware that fasting (*bigu* 辟穀) for *neidan* practice is an involved process and it should be guided by an experienced teacher.

- Practice with a full bladder.
  - o If we practice in the morning, Wang Liping recommends not relieving ourselves first. I am not sure why, but perhaps it increases the internal pressure of the lower abdominal cavity.

- Retreat.
  - o Withdrawing from the noise and bustle of our world also works wonders for *neidan* practice. The *xiatian* is a quiet, subtle, and delicate thing; it is easily overlooked when our mind and bodies are caught up in the rush of modern life.

- Simplify life.
  - o I once asked a Tibetan Buddhist monk how to enter deeper states of stillness. He provided two simple and direct answers: "First, you have to want to, and second, simplify your life." The same applies to finding the *xiatian*. If our life is too busy and hectic, then our *shen* energy scatters and it will be harder to gather it inside the body.

- Relax and empty body.
  - o First relax and then empty the body, especially the inside of the torso.

- Transmission.
  - o It is extremely helpful, and some might even claim essential, to practice sitting with a teacher who is regulating the energy field and directing our *shen* while we work through the methods.

- Regular practice.
  - o As a general rule, the more we can practice the better—at least once a day is important. But overdoing it will not help either, so find balance.

- *Youwei* and *wuwei*.
  - o Find a balance between *youwei* and *wuwei* in your practice. For example, too much doing (*youwei*) and it will not work; too much being (*wuwei*) will not help either. If anything, I find it best to err on the side of *wuwei*. Therefore, try to do lots of silent sitting, both integrated into the sessions as well as entire sessions of just silent sitting.

- Seal off Three Lower Yin Gates properly.
  - o The three lower gates include the genitals, *huiyin*, and anus. Follow the methods in Chapter 6 to seal them up.

- Seal off the human universe (including seven upper openings) properly.
  - o It is easier to gather the *shen* and focus inside the torso when the body is energetically sealed up. I find pore breathing to be the best method for this. The Taoists correlate sealing up the seven upper openings (our sense organs) to putting the lid on the pot. Once we prepare the cauldron, the lid needs to go on for the cooking process. Again, refer to the Yinxian Methods in Chapter 6.

PART FOUR

Supplemental Practices

12.

Taoist Walking

Sitting cross-legged in meditation is not the only way to do *neidan*. We can also practice while walking, standing, and lying down. The Taoists say that movement cultivates energy channels, standing cultivates energy meridians, sitting cultivates *shen* and *yi*, and lying cultivates *ling* 靈 (the everlasting energetic part of us). The following chapters will present a range of supplemental practices. If you are getting bored sitting around all day, here is a chance to try something different.

The supplemental practices include Taoist Walking, Standing Post Practice, Tree Practice, and Sleeping Practice. Each of these practices contains a wealth of methods, and each require a lifetime of study to fully understand.

Taoist Walking is an ancient method for exchanging energy with nature. In Chinese, the method is called the Nature Qi Exchange Method (*ziran huan qi fa* 自然換氣法). This meditative method progresses through three levels and nine methods. Each stage uses Taoist techniques for coordinating our breath, body, mind, spirit, and *qi* with brisk walking. While maintaining a vigorous pace, we learn to connect into the environment around us in profound ways.

Taoist Walking leaves one feeling refreshed and clean. Imagine opening the windows of a house that have been shut up for too long. We bring *qi* from our environment into our body and release any stagnant stuff locked inside. Of course, any walk in nature could have a similar effect. What is different and deeper about Taoist Walking is the techniques we use to amplify the effect.

I also really like Taoist Walking for its exercise value. We are walking at a brisk pace for a good hour. Wang Liping recommends 5 to 10 kilometres. Although shorter distances are okay, it takes time each session for the practice to open up, and each session has various stages through which to progress. Strength and stamina are very helpful for *neidan* practice. In order to sit for long sessions, our physical body needs to be in good shape, especially when we begin forming the elixir. The elixir creates a lot of energetic pressure inside the body that we need to hold. Exercise helps. Why should we do normal exercise when we can exercise the Taoist way!

I also find the Nature Qi Exchange Method considerably helps with our breath work. Coordinating breath with our steps allows an easy way to slow down our breathing. Extending our breath is important for *neidan*, and Taoist Walking works well for this. Walking also helps to relax the diaphragm, which in turn facilitates our breathing.

Another effect of Taoist Walking is to assist Taoist practitioners with breaking out of their own bodies. When we start practicing *neidan*, we seek to seal the physical body, creating a body with no energetic leaks. This is vital for *neidan*. But at a certain point in our training we need to get out of the physical body and energetically connect with the world around us. It then becomes time for Taoist Walking.

There are different ways to do Taoist Walking. The practice includes three levels, called vehicles, and nine methods. Below you will find Level One.

The Three Vehicles (Levels)

Level One: Lower Vehicle (*xia cheng* 下乘) is for our health and wellbeing. The first level works to prevent and cure illness and extend our years.

1. Method for Expelling and Ingesting *Qi* (*xingbu tuna fa* 步吐納法).
2. Method for Sealing *Qi* (*xingbu biqi fa* 行步閉氣法).
3. Method for Ingesting Substance (*xingbu nazhi fa* 行步納質法).

Level Two: Middle Vehicle (*zhong cheng* 中乘) is for returning to the source.

1. Method for Expelling Substance (*xingbu tuzhi fa* 行步吐質法).
2. Method for Restoring *Qi* (*xingbu buqi fa* 行步布質法).
3. Method for Fenju (*xingbu fenju fa* 行步分局法).

Level Three: Upper Vehicle (*shang cheng* 上乘) is for merging with heaven to become one with all.

1. Method for Opening our Meridians (*xingbu tongjing fa* 步通經法).
2. Method for Transmitting Ling (*xingbu chuanling fa* 行步傳靈法).
3. Method for Hiding the Body (*xingbu yinshen fa* 行步隱身法).

Level One

Level One has three methods. Each method follows the same sequence of practice, the only difference is the breathing. For all three methods of Level One, a session will progress through the same six stages. At each stage, we coordinate our breathing with our steps. We inhale for a set number of steps, and exhale for the same amount. The set number is either 3, 6, 12, or 24 depending on our breathing capability. For methods two and three we also hold our breath at certain points for the same number of steps as the inhale and exhale.

Method for Expelling and Ingesting *Qi*: inhale and exhale.

Method for Sealing *Qi*: inhale – pause – exhale.

Method for Ingesting Substance: inhale – pause – exhale – pause.

Coordinating breath with our steps is the baseline of the practice. If we get lost in the practice or drift off into random thinking, we can come back to counting our steps with the inhale and exhale. Without coordinating the breath with the stepping, the rest of the practice will not open up.

In the first stage of Level One, we start coordinating breath with our steps as we regulate gentle nose breathing. Then in the next few stages, we use the breath to focus our *yinian* and bring our *shen* into the body. Both *yi* and *shen* can piggyback onto the breath to get inside the torso. Once the *shen* and *yi* are inside, we can work on certain areas to move and transform *qi,* all of which are completed in time with our quick stride. The areas split into six stages. We sequentially work the nose, mouth, lungs, stomach/spleen, *xiatian*, and body pores. A session can last any length of time, though for best results consider walking for at least 45 minutes. An hour is even better.

Another way of doing Taoist Walking is just doing Stages 1 and 6, thus skipping going inside with Stages 2 to 5. Start by regulating nose breathing and then move directly to body pore breathing. Beginners find this method particularly beneficial. Working inside the body can be a little discombobulating. Working only with our body pores keeps the practice simple. For the first few years of teaching Taoist Walking, Wang Liping would only teach the body pore method.

Stage 1: Nose Breathing

1. Look: look afar, both eyes look at a level gaze to the horizon.

2. Walk: walk at a brisk pace.

3. Posture: walk like you are pregnant with belly sticking out a bit, chest open, and arms swinging back and forth.

4. Breathing: coordinate inhale and exhale with your steps by counting to either 3, 6, 12, or 24 for each inhale and each exhale.

5. Nose: focus *yinian* on the air going in and out of your nose.

6. Exchange: pure *qi* from surrounding natural environment comes into body with your breath; turbid *qi* returns to the environment with your breath.

Stage 2: Mouth

1. Focus *yinian* inside mouth.

2. Breathe in, focus on air in the mouth. Breathe out, focus on air in the mouth. (Do not focus on where the air comes from; instead, just place *yinian* in the mouth).

Stage 3: Lungs

1. Focus *yinian* on breath in lungs.

2. Breathe in, gently contract lungs; breathe out, gently expand lungs.

3. Feel the whole of the lungs fill up with air and *yinian*.

4. Breathe in and out completely, working the whole lung, but stay relaxed.

5. Lungs should begin to feel heavy.

Optional: slightly contract and expand rib cage with breathing.

Optional: work one lung at a time.

Stage 4: Stomach/spleen

1. Focus *yinian* on stomach/spleen area.

2. Breathe in, stomach/spleen contract; breathe out, stomach/spleen expand.

3. Walking speeds up a little at this stage, so we might need more time to regulate.

4. Breathe out through mouth, not nose; mouth is slightly open.

5. Breathe out turbid *qi* from stomach. This is especially good to do first thing in the morning after turbid *qi* has built up in the stomach over the night.

Stage 5: *Xiatian*

1. Focus *yinian* on *xiatian*.

2. Breathe in, *xiaofu* contracts; breathe out, *xiaofu* expands.

3. Use *xiaofu* breathing to pull up and seal genitals and anus.

4. After a while, shift movement from *xiaofu* to *xiatian*; outside of *xiaofu* does not move.

Stage 6: Pore Breathing

1. Focus *yinian* on whole body pores.

2. Breathe in, pores contract; breathe out, pores expand.

3. Bring *qi* from the environment through body pores into *xiatian*, release the body through body pores into the environment.

Advanced:

1. When breathing out, expand your energy field away from the body as a sphere. See how far you can go.

Practice Points

- Properly coordinate breathing with stepping
- Properly use *yinian*
- Avoid random thoughts
- Walk at least 5 kilometres
- Walk quickly

13.

Standing Post Practice

Standing still and upright with arms and hands arrayed in various positions has been a fixture of Taoist practice for many centuries. Standing post (*zhanzhuang* 站椿) is another supplemental practice used in Dragon Gate training. To do standing post practice, stand in a specific static posture and enter a meditative state. As with sitting meditation, we can use techniques or we can simply enter stillness. I have found through my own practice that standing post practice works well for learning how to relax and sink the body; it also offers a way to cultivate *qi*.

There are two main approaches to standing post practice: training tendons or developing *qi*. Training tendons is more difficult and requires the guidance of an experienced teacher. Unlike in the West, in neigong training, tendons refer to all the long tissues and sinews in the body. To train the tendons with standing post practice the body must be positioned and worked very specifically. In addition, there is a specific process the student goes through to allow the tissues of the body to open up and become fully engaged in the posture. This sort of training also enhances *qi* circulation. Because the standing post training can be challenging to explain in a book, this chapter will focus on how to do standing post to develop *qi*.

The Dragon Gate system uses nine different postures and a variety of internal methods. In this book, I will share the first posture and three levels of internal practice. The internal methods are similar to when we sit. In some ways, standing practice provides an opportunity for us to work on the same old stuff but from a different angle.

The Sit

Understanding how to sit while also standing is vital to standing practice. Here, I am not referring to sitting meditation. When we sit in a chair, our pelvis and tailbone align in a certain way to allow the sit bones to bear the weight of our torso.

When doing standing practice, we also want this same alignment. We want the sit bones pointing down. To stand properly we need to learn how to sit while standing. To do this imagine we are sitting on a high stool. Notice what happens to the tailbone and pelvic area when we do this, and especially pay attention to the groin area or what the Chinese call the *kua* 胯.

To stand properly we need to utilize the *kua*. The *kua* is located in the vicinity of the groin area. We have a *kua* on both left and right sides. The *kua* includes all the tendons and muscles that run through the groin area (inguinal crease). There are a number of tendons and muscles that run down the inside of the thigh and run upwards attaching to the pelvic bowl and lower spine. All of this area is considered part of the *kua*. In standing and moving *neigong* practices, understanding how to properly use our *kua* is vital to the development of internal skill. To use the *kua*, start with the high sit and then relax the *kua*, the lower down and deeper inside the *kua*, the better. There should be a sense of relaxing down the inside of the thigh all the way into the ground.

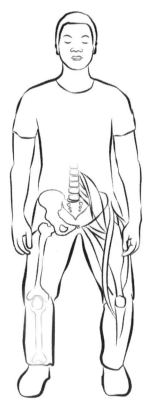

Kua

Wuji Posture

The Wuji Posture (*wuji zhuang* 無極樁) is the first posture we use in Dragon Gate practice.

Posture:

1. Feet shoulder width, legs slightly bent (not too low, an inch lower than normal is fine).

2. Arms naturally hang at sides, relax shoulders, sink shoulder blades, and relax chest.

3. Palms face inwards, fingers slightly bent.

4. Sink into *kua*, tailbone aligned, relax whole body and sit as if sitting on a high stool.

5. Mouth ready: lips closed, teeth lightly touching, tongue touches upper palate.

6. Top of head slightly extended upwards.

7. Chin slightly tucked in.

Preparation:

1. Look to horizon, bring *shenguang* back to edge of human universe.

2. Eyes closed or open (unless doing after tree practice, then eyes closed).

Level One—Pore Breathing

1. Preparation: First breathe naturally to settle the mind and *shen*

2. Breathe in, *qi* from all directions, compress into whole body pores
   Breathe out, *qi* from whole body pores, release into surroundings
   (Repeat 24x)

3. Natural breathing for as long as you like

Level Two—Pore Breathing and Inner Breathing

1. Preparation: First breathe naturally to settle the mind and *shen*

2. Breathe in,
   (outer) *qi* from all directions, compress into whole body pores;
   (inner) *qi* past navel
   Breathe out,
   (outer) *qi* from whole body pores, release into surroundings;
   (inner) *qi* not past heart

3. Natural breathing for as long as you like

Level Three—Sphere Breathing

1. Preparation: First breathe naturally to settle the mind and *shen*

2. Breathe in,
   (outer) natural cosmic *qi* becomes a sphere and compresses into whole body pores;
   (inner) whole body pores compress towards *xiatian*, while at same time contract *xiaofu*
   Breathe out,
   (outer) *qi* from whole body pores, *qi* expand towards horizon;
   (inner) *qi* from *xiatian* expand towards the whole body pores

3. Natural breathing for as long as you like

14

Balancing Practice (Tree Practice)

Balancing Practice (*pingheng gong* 平衡功) teaches us how to work directly with another energy field (*qichang* 氣場). All living organisms have energy fields. With Balancing Practice, we exchange energy and information with another plant, animal, or person. Since trees tend to be the easiest to work with because they are big and stationary, we will focus exclusively on Tree Practice in this chapter. The Dragon Gate Lineage uses various methods and movements to set up a relationship with the tree in order to exchange energy and information. The exchange teaches us how to harmonize with another field and how to project and receive *qi*. The practice is also good for health and leaves us feeling calm and rejuvenated.

To work with a tree as Balancing Practice, we use standing post practice combined with moving postures and methods. The Dragon Gate Lineage has nine moving postures and numerous methods. Six of the postures use stationary footwork and three require moving footwork. Only the first five postures are included here. The movements of the last fixed posture and the moving postures are too complex to describe in writing, so they are best learned directly from a teacher.

Caution

- It is best not to do tree practice during the day, except under certain conditions.

- We should avoid using the practices in this chapter on other people unless we know what we are doing. Tree Practice is how we learn to emit *qi*. Emitting *qi* can be used for both healing or harming. When we work with a tree and there are other people about, be careful not to emit *qi* into them.

Five Phases and Trees

Trees have *qi* and different trees have different kinds of *qi*. Trees and their *qi* are classified according to the Five Phases. Colour is the simplest way to find the phase of a tree. Working with trees can be excellent for our health, especially if we want to rebalance the *qi* of one organ in particular. Understanding the Five Phase colours is most important because it tells us what colour of *qi* to use during the practice.

Five Phases	Metal	Wood	Water	Fire	Earth
Five Colours	White	Green	Blue/Black	Red	Yellow
Five Organs	Lungs	Liver	Kidneys	Heart	Spleen
Five Trees	Poplar	Pine	Cypress	Chinese Parasol/ Apple Tree	Willow

The Session

Complete each session of the Tree Practice in three parts:

1. Preparation

2. Paired Practice

3. Standing Post Practice

Preparation calms our body and mind and connects us with the tree. Paired practice is where we apply the methods and movement, which will vary depending on what we are doing. Then we turn our back on the tree and stand. This is similar to how *neidan* sessions progress: first, we prepare; second, we do something; third, we wait in stillness and see what happens.

Preparation

All nine methods of tree practice begin with the following preparation.

1. Stand in front of the tree in standing post posture, one arm's length from the tree

2. Become still and relaxed

3. Look at the tree with eyes wide open

4. Close eyes and think about the tree, while quietly sending your greetings to the tree

Once you get a handle on the above four basic preparation steps, you can add some additional steps as well.

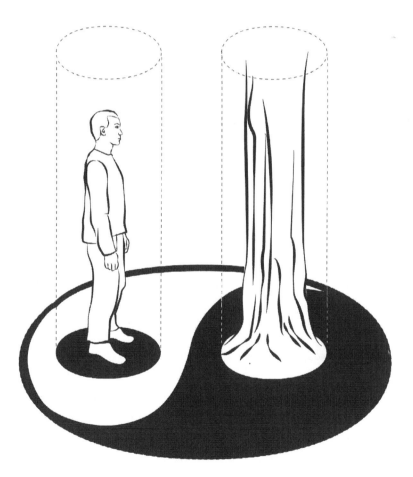

Standing with a tree

Optional Steps:

1. With eyes closed, though advanced practitioners can do with eyes wide open, look forward and observe the shape and colour of the tree. The colour should match one of the Five Phases. Then intentionally plot out the *qi* field of the tree. The tree's field will be cylindrical—imagine above is heaven and below is earth.

2. Now intentionally plot out your own *qi* field. Make it also cylindrical and of the same colour as the tree.

3. Bring the *shenguang* into the body and start regulating the breath. Breathe out, expand our *qi* field to gradually include the tree's *qi* field. Breathe in, expand the tree's *qi* field to gradually include our *qi* field.

   Make breathing even, deep, fine, and long. Continue until we feel that we have melted together as one with the tree, until our body and limbs feel swollen. Once this happens, we may start the practice.

Paired Practice

After the preparation period is over, we begin the active part of Paired Practice. We begin working with movement, breath, and intention to exchange *qi* with the tree. We do this for as long as we like. The various postures are detailed below. More than one posture can be used in each session. Feel free to mix and match depending what you are in the mood for.

Closing: Standing Post Practice

Now we turn our back to the tree and stand. Standing with our back to the tree is where we absorb the most *qi*. This is an important part of the practice. Remember to stand for an equal length of time or greater as the time we used for the movements; otherwise, we might end up feeling depleted. Standing is best done with our eyes closed and focused within our bodies. Consult Chapter 13 on standing practice for deeper instruction. We may use the Wuji Posture or Baoyuan Posture (see future volume).

Wang Liping also recommends doing Five Phase Organ Practice with hand movements. This is a great opportunity to run the tree *qi* through our organs. If you feel like being more hands on with the closing, try it out. Here is the sequence:

1. Look down to *xiatian*

2. Do *xiaofu* breathing until warm or hot

3. Do Five Phase Organ Practice 3x, 6x, or 12x

Method

Posture 1: Both Hands Pull Up and Down

Posture 1

Movement and Breath

Stretch hands straight out in front of you, keeping some space under the armpits, with the elbows bent. Hands should be positioned vertically, with thumbs being the highest and pinky fingers the lowest. Face palms to the centre of tree. The line between the two palms and the centre of the tree should form a triangle, with a 90-degree angle where the two lines meet in the tree.

Next, begin moving in an up-and-down squatting motion. The two palms move up and down level with the tree trunk following your squatting movement. As you squat down, bend wrists so that the fingers point upwards; as you go up, the wrists bend so that the fingers point downwards.

There are two acupoints on the wrist that need to be sealed. One is on top where the base of the thumb meets the wrist. The other is at the bottom in line with the pinky finger. As you squat down, angle hands upwards to seal the acupoint on top of the wrist. As you move up, angle the hands downwards to seal the acupoint on the bottom of the wrist. At the bottom of the movement, the hands do not move past the knees. Meanwhile, the top of the hands do not go past the eyebrows. The spine remains straight and perpendicular. Squat as low as your age, health, and level of ability determine.

When you breathe in, both hands pull upwards. When you breathe out, both hands pull downwards. Keep the movement circular, without stopping anywhere, and regulate the breathing step by step to be even, deep, fine, and long. Start with six times per minute. Then work towards going slower, such as one time per minute. Wang Liping teaches that if we can keep it going for three hours, we will definitely feel the *qi* moving!

Intention

In the beginning, feel free to use visualization to get things going. But be aware of the difference between imagination and actually using *qi*.

Level One:

Breathe in, draw *qi* from the roots of the tree through the palms into the body and pull up, almost as if pulling the tree out of the ground.

Breathe out, emit *qi* from your palms to hit the tree at one point. You can choose to put this point at the centre of the tree, the back of the tree, or even penetrate straight through the tree and into another tree.

Level Two:

Breathe in, draw *qi* from the tree into your body through the body pores.
Breathe out, emit *qi* from palms to one point (see Level One).

Level Three:

Breathe in, draw *qi* from the tree entering the body through the palms, up the inner side of the arms, through the shoulders and then down into the *xiaofu*.

Breathe out, lead *qi* from *xiaofu* to follow the belt meridian to the back of the body, from the *mingmen* 命門 area on the lower back, up to the shoulders, and from the shoulders the *qi* splits and goes down the arms and out the palms into the tree.

Throughout the practice our intention needs to be strong, determined, and resolute. We need to maintain the sense that the tree in front of us is a certain coloured pillar of *qi*. The *qi* coming out of our palms is the same colour as the tree. Establish a balance with the tree, a balance of *qi* and information between us and the tree.

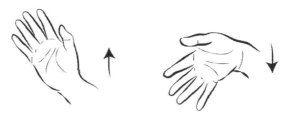

Posture 1 hand position

Posture 2: Slice Vertically with Ten Fingers

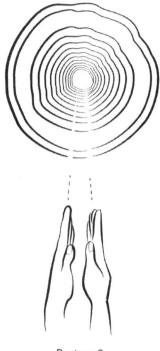

Posture 2

Movement and Breath

Stretch hands close together straight out in front of you, with elbows bent. Hands are positioned vertically palm facing palm one inch apart.

As with Posture One, begin the squatting movement in coordination with the arms. At the bottom of the movement, the hands do not move past the knees; at the top, the arms do not go past the level of the shoulders. As you move up, your fingertips droop down. As you move down, your fingertips turn upwards. The spine is straight and centred throughout.

When you breathe in, the hands move up. When you breathe out, the hands move down. Try to make breathing very circular by breathing even, deep, fine, and long.

Intention

Imagine lines of *qi* coming out of the fingertips, cutting thin strips into the tree. The thinner the lines, the better. The lines of *qi* are the same colour as the energy field of the tree.

Posture 3: Slice Horizontally with Ten Fingers

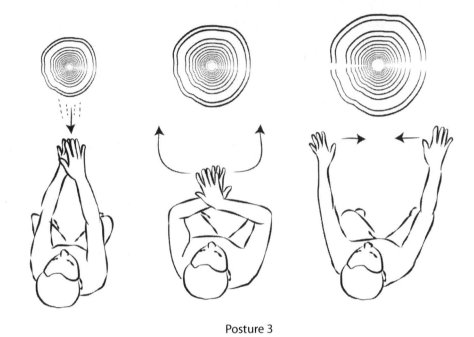

Posture 3

Movement and Breath

Begin with the arms and hands extended outwards in front of the chest. Palms face down. Breathe in, draw hands towards the chest as they cross over each other. Hold breath as hands split apart to either side, and extend towards tree on either side, moving horizontally from the sides towards centre of tree. Breathe out, as the tips of the fingers move in front of the tree. Palms remain facing down throughout the entire movement.

Squat lower while holding the breath and repeat. We may change our level as we squat up and down, moving where we cut through the tree. I usually choose three levels and alternate between them. The highest level will be with my legs almost fully extended, and the lowest with my thighs more parallel to the ground.

Intention

When breathing in, draw *qi* from the tree in through the fingertips (advanced variation is through the body pores). When breathing out, cut a thin strip through the tree using *qi* from fingertips. Focus your intention to cut the tree. Imagine *qi* from your fingertips matching the colour of the tree.

Posture 4: Push with Palms

Movement and Breath

Start with arms and hands extended towards the tree at chest height, with palms facing the ground. Breathe in, bend arms, and draw hands towards the chest, while fingers continue to face the tree. Breathe out, bend wrists to ninety degrees (fingers face sky), and make pushing motion towards the tree with your palms.

Squat lower when inhaling and repeat. We may change our level a number of times as we squat up and down, moving where we push the tree. We only move up or down when we inhale. I usually choose three levels and alternate between them. The highest level will be with my legs almost fully extended, and the lowest with my thighs more parallel to the ground.

Intention

Imagine tree as a pillar of coloured *qi* that we push and pull with our movements.

Posture 5: Sword Form

Posture 5 hand position

The body movement and breathing are the same as in Posture Two, but with a different hand position. Make the sword-form hand posture: index finger and middle finger extended, ring and little finger curled back, thumb over the nail of the ring finger. Stand in position facing the tree. Breathe in, stand and raise arms with hands bent downwards. Breathe out, squat and lower arms with hands bent upwards. Use intention to slice the tree on exhale. You can also do horizontal movements as in Posture Three, or simply face the tree in a horse stance, while pointing your middle finger at the tree, exhaling, and emiting *qi* to make an energetic hole in the tree. Be careful to not inadvertently use this on another person or animal unless you know what you are doing.

15.

Sleep Practice

Despite its name, Sleep Practice (*shuigong* 睡功) is not about sleeping. We are simply using the supine position to practice. In the old days, this practice was called Sleeping Immortal Practice (*shuixian gong* 睡仙功). Sleeping Practice is surprisingly powerful. Practicing while lying down works the body in different ways than sitting. The position is particularly beneficial for replenishing and nourishing *qi*. There are neigong lineages in China that rely only on using a supine position to build up *qi*. It is also one of the few ways to replenish *ling* 靈, a subtle spiritual energy related to *shen* (see future volumes).

The sleeping practice of the Dragon Gate Lineage uses eleven body postures. Nine are detailed below. Each posture has specific body position requirements. For example, sometimes the hands lay at our sides with the palms facing down, while another position will have the palms facing up. Each body posture also includes different stages of practice and several versions. A usual session will last an hour or more.

Instructions

1. Lay on your back with legs straight and feet shoulder width apart. Feet may be slightly splayed with the top of the feet naturally falling to either side. The whole body is straight and relaxed. Use a pillow for the head if needed.

2. With eyes open, look straight up as far as possible.

3. Bring *shenguang* back to between the eyebrows.

4. Gently close eyes (eyes stay closed for the rest of session).

5. Bring *yinian* to a location in the body that you will be working on for that posture (ignore this for Posture Nine).

a. Go down outside of torso to location (for beginners).

b. Bring into head and send it down the internal centreline to the location (for more advanced practitioners).

6. Follow breathing instructions for each posture.
   Breathing should be fine, deep, and long. Repeat 24x

7. Return to natural breathing.

8. Stay focused inside the body for the rest of the session and observe the changes.

The Nine Postures

	Posture Name	Body Position	Location of Work
1	Calm the *Shen*	Palms face down, arms straight alongside the body	1. Whole body pores 2. *Xiaofu* 3. *Xiatian*
2	Lower and Regulate Blood Pressure	Legs together, fully extended, heels touching, top of feet naturally splay slightly outwards in a 'V' shape	1. Start at bottom of feet, inhale up through centre of legs to *xiatian* 2. Go in opposite direction
3	Preserve *Jing* and Support Blood	Palms face down, one over the other, on the *zhongji* acupoint	*zhongji* acupoint: Four *cun* 'thumb' widths below navel on centreline of body
4	Return *Yang* to Strengthen	Palms face down, one over the other, on the *qihai* acupoint	*qihai* acupoint: 1.5 *cun* 'thumb' widths below navel on centreline of body
5	Replenish Deficiency by Returning *Yang*	Palms face down, one over the other, on the *shenque* acupoint	*shenque* acupoint: centre of navel
6	Regulate *Qi* to Support the Heart	Palms face down, one over the other, on the *tanzhong* acupoint	*tanzhong* acupoint: midway between nipples on sternum

7	Protect the Liver, Clear the Gallbladder	Palms face down, one over the other, on the liver area, while propping left elbow up on pillow	Liver
8	Support the Spleen, Strengthen the Stomach	Palms face down, one over the other, on the stomach/spleen area, while propping right elbow up on pillow	Stomach/Spleen
9	Peace and Happiness	Palms face up, arms straight alongside the body	Celestial eye. 1. Between eyebrow 2. Upper Field 3. Rear Celestial Mirror

Note: Use pillows, if necessary, to prop up elbows, especially for Postures Seven and Eight.

Practice Tips

1. Do not move. During a session, the body might begin to feel numb, itchy, full, or as if we just need to move. This is *qi* opening up our channels and if we move, we lose the opportunity for them to open up.

2. Do not sleep. Stay awake.

3. Use Inner Seeing. With eyes closed, look at the area you are working on. A trick to doing this is to look at your nose first, and from your nose watch the area.

4. Use Inner Hearing. Listen to the area you are working on.

5. Practice in a different place from where you sleep. This is not necessary, but it can help to stay awake.

6. Change body position after a sleep practice session, before you go to sleep. At the very least, roll over onto your side. This turns off the *qi*.

7. No random thoughts.

8. Lie comfortably.

Posture 1: Calm the *Shen*

Calming the Shen Posture (*an shen shi* 安神式) is the first and most commonly used position in Sleep Practice. Calming the *Shen* is good for rejuvenation of the body and spirit. It replenishes *jing* energy and calms our *shen*. The posture benefits those who work hard with either their body or their mind. If you are feeling depleted, then give this one a try. There are several variations for this posture. I have listed a couple below.

Guided Instructions

> **Version 1a:** outside to pores to *xiaofu*, starting with inhale.
>> Inhale, *qi* from all directions compress through whole body pores into *xiaofu* cavity.
>> Exhale, *qi* from *xiaofu* cavity releases through body pores into surroundings.

> **Version 1b:** outside to pores to *xiaofu*, starting with exhale.
>> Exhale, *qi* from *xiaofu* cavity releases through body pores into surroundings.
>> Inhale, *qi* from all directions compress through whole body pores into *xiaofu* cavity.

> **Version 2a:** pores to *xiatian*, starting with inhale.
>> Inhale, *qi* from body pores contract into *xiatian*.
>> Exhale, *qi* from *xiatian* expand to body pores (do not leave body).

> **Version 2b:** pores to *xiatian*, starting with exhale.
>> Exhale, *qi* from *xiatian* expand to body pores (do not leave body).
>> Inhale, *qi* from body pores contract into *xiatian*.

> **Versions 3, 4, and 5:** contract/expand *xiatian, xiaofu,* or Inner Cavity (see future volume). Can start on inhale or exhale for either.
>> Breathe in, contract *xiatian* (or *xiaofu* or Inner Cavity).
>> Breathe out, *xiatian* expand (or *xiaofu* or Inner Cavity).

Posture 2: Lower and Regulate Blood Pressure

As the name suggests, this posture lowers and regulates blood pressure. The posture is also good for opening up the *qi* channels of the legs. I also find this posture works surprisingly well for alleviating leg soreness after long hours of sitting.

To get best results stay very focused and coordinate the breath, the eyes, and movement of *yinian* and *qi* through the legs. Slowly move the *yinian* and *qi* up and down the leg following your breath and using your eyes.

Guided Instructions

Version 1a: To start with inhale, first look at and bring *yinian* to bottom of feet.

> Inhale, slowly draw *qi* from bottom of feet up
> > legs into *xiatian*.
>
> Exhale, slowly push *qi* from *xiatian* through legs
> > out bottom of feet.

Version 1b: To start with exhale, first look at and bring *yinian* to *xiatian*.

> Breathe in, slowly push *qi* from *xiatian* through
> > legs out bottom of feet.
>
> Breathe out, slowly draw *qi* from bottom of feet
> > up legs into *xiatian*.

Postures 3 to 6

Postures Three through Six work to open certain acupoints along the *Ren* Meridian. The *Ren* Meridian runs down the front centreline of the body and is part of the Microcosmic Orbit. These four postures help to open the Microcosmic Orbit, as well as having other uses.

Place both hands palms down, one over the other, face down on the acupoint in question. These four acupoints are found along the external centreline of the body (*zhongxin xian* 中心線). By breathing into and out of these points, we seek to transform the *qi* (*qihua*) in the area.

Guided Instructions

Version 1a: outside body to acupoint, starting with inhale.

Breathe in, *qi* from all directions compress
into acupoint.
Breathe out, *qi* from acupoint release through
body into surroundings.

Version 1b: outside body to acupoint, starting with exhale.

Breathe out, *qi* from acupoint release through
body into surroundings.
Breathe in, *qi* from all directions compress into acupoint.

Version 2a: pores to acupoint, starting with inhale.

Breathe in, pull from whole body pores to acupoint.
Breathe out, *qi* from acupoint releases to whole body
pores, but does not go out.

Version 2b: pores to acupoint, starting with exhale.

Breathe out, *qi* from acupoint releases to
whole body pores, but does not go out.
Breathe in, pull from whole body pores to
acupoint.

Posture 3: Preserve *Jing* and Support Blood

Posture Three works the *zhongji* acupoint, which is four cun "thumb-width" below the navel along centreline of body. This posture is good for preserving *jing* and supporting the blood. It is also good for bladder health and balancing out the *qi* between the *Chong* Meridian (Thrusting Meridian) and the *Ren* Meridian.

Posture 4: Return *Yang* to Strengthen

Posture Four works the *qihai* acupoint, which is 1.5 cun "thumb-width" below the navel along the centreline of body. This posture is good for kidney deficiency and *qi* stagnation. It also helps with irregular menstruation and impotence.

Posture 5: Return *Yang* to Replenish

Posture Five works the *shenque* acupoint at the centre of the navel. The *shenque* acupoint is important for organ health and overall vitality. In the old days they'd say, "our body has a navel, just as the heavens have the pole star." Working this point warms the *yang qi* to replenish our body. It also cleans out our digestion and removes stagnation from the internal organs. This posture is good to practice when we are feeling tired and worn out. It can also help to open the *mingmen* area 命門 on the lower back.

Posture 6: Regulate *Qi* to Enhance Heart

Posture Six works the *tanzhong* point on the sternum between the nipples. The *tanzhong* area and chest cavity is connected with our emotions and is a good posture to help smooth out any emotional instability issues such as depression or phobias. If you are feeling a little out of sorts, give this one a try. This posture is also useful for lung and heart related illnesses, as well as activating and transforming *qi* in the *zhongtian* (Middle Field) itself.

Postures 7 and 8

These two postures work the liver/gallbladder and the stomach/spleen. Posture Seven, Protect Liver and Clear Gallbladder, works the liver and gallbladder, which are on the right side of the body. Posture Eight, Strengthen Stomach and Spleen, works the stomach/spleen on the left. To work these organs, we cover them with our palms and use pillows to support the elbows if needed.

Guided Instructions

> Breathe in, *qi* compresses into organ.
> Breathe out, *qi* comes up and out of mouth
>   (tongue touches lower gums).

Posture 9: Peace and Happiness

This posture works the Celestial Eye (*tianmu* 天目). The body position is the same as the Posture One except that the palms face upwards to the sky. Celestial Eye practice is a central feature of Dragon Gate *neidan* training and will be detailed in future volumes. The Celestial Eye is located between the eyebrows and extends inside the head. I include the practice in this volume for completeness, but I recommend not trying this posture if you have not learned celestial eye practice.

There are at least six different ways of doing Posture Nine. I will only include the first two. The others all involve working within the head cavity, which can be dangerous. The brain is a finely-tuned machine, and it is best that we do not mess around inside until we know what we are doing.

Posture Nine requires a different approach than the others. After the opening sequence, we bring the *shenguang* and *yinian* back to between the eyebrows like we normally do. Instead of going to another location, however, we stay between the eyebrows.

Guided Instructions

Version 1a: celestial space to between eyebrows, starting with exhale.
Breathe out, expand point from between eyebrows
upwards and outwards to the sky going far.
Breathe in, bring *yinian* back to between eyebrows
(but not inside head).

On the 24th time, finish on the exhale, when our *yinian*
is expanded outwards. Return to natural breathing,
and with eyes closed observe the changes in the
celestial space.

Version 1b: celestial space to between eyebrows, starting with inhale.
Breathe out, expand point from between eyebrows
upwards and outwards to the sky going far.
Breathe in, bring *yinian* back to between eyebrows
(but not inside head).

PART FIVE

Entering the Gate, continued

16.

Training with Wang Liping, Part Two

Fall 2014

A month before I left for Southeast Asia, a red inflamed sore appeared over my right eyelid. A few days into the intensive, the sore finally burst, releasing pus. A couple days later, another sore grew above my other eyelid and lasted several months. I asked Wang Liping if this was "liver fire" releasing. According to classical Chinese medicine, anger can manifest as heat in the liver, an organ associated with the eyes. Wang Liping told me not to think so much.

The day my Microcosmic Orbit opened in Southeast Asia, I pulled my left abductor, a muscle in the groin area that runs down the inside of the thigh. Austria had been all about my right hip, but now it was my left hip that was going through changes. When I returned to Vancouver, I cut back on the long sitting sessions, reducing my training schedule to two 45 to 60 minute sessions a day until my left hip healed. It took a few months. Although I was a little frustrated, I had to trust the process.

In mid-October of that year, I began tuning into a pulse inside my body. I noticed a noise within my body about forty-five minutes into a sitting session. Becoming very still, I focused on the sound and realized that it was actually a very fast pulsing movement inside my torso. The more I tuned into the pulse, the more it spread and filled my body. It was quite comfortable, but not as overpowering as the vibration I experienced in Southeast Asia. Over the next few days, the pulsing began to activate my governing channel up my spine, starting at my perineum (*huiyin*) and running to the crown of the head (*baihui*). The whole channel felt tingly and full.

I finally had a breakthrough after several days of allowing this pulsing to open up. While focusing on the movement, I had a random thought about the lack of systemized training for Westerners undertaking Taoist ordination at the White

Cloud Temple in Beijing. I realized that people need to take care of the training themselves. The gates are all there; it is up to us as individuals to open them. This realization squared directly with the issues of frustration I had been processing in previous months. This anger had kept me from taking responsibility for myself and my life. As soon as I had this epiphany, a rush of *qi* shot down my left leg and filled it with an intense pulsing sensation. The pain in my left groin subsided and the redness in the sore over my eye reduced after I finished the session. Within a few days, the length of my sitting sessions increased dramatically. My left hip was healing.

Three days after this insight, I felt a bubbling sensation in my lower abdominal cavity during an evening session. I woke up at 2:30 that morning with a migraine and strong nausea. Although I slept fitfully for the rest of the night, I woke up feeling surprisingly rejuvenated.

The next intensive with Wang Liping was scheduled for November, and I was working hard to increase the length of my sits. Although my left leg had started to heal, I continued to purge turbid *qi*, which most commonly was released through the sole of my foot. I started making an involuntary high-pitched whining sound during some sessions. The sound became very loud (my poor neighbours!), and my left leg just kept on vibrating, right to its centre.

Korea, November 2014

My third intensive with Wang Liping took place in Korea. The Korean group is well established and is one of the oldest international groups practicing with Wang Liping. Each year, its members organize two intensives with Wang Liping. They also arrange two to three additional training events with Quan Guanhua, a close student of Wang Liping, who also serves as the group's translator (he is fluent in both Mandarin and Korean). They are incredibly open and supportive. I trained alongside them four times over the next two years. I remember my time with them fondly.

In Korea, I was reminded of what Wang Liping innocuously calls "adding pressure." During sessions, Wang Liping regulates the *qi* field in the room, helping practitioners open their meridians and clear turbid *qi*. I started to feel the pressure during the second session as it bore down on my head, arms, and legs. I found it difficult to maintain my chosen posture under the encumbrance of this intense energetic weight. It was much different from practicing at home. Although I had been sitting the same amount in the weeks leading up to the intensive, I was exhausted after only my second session in Korea. The Taoists call this having a tired spirit (*shenlei* 神累). My body and mind were fine, but the fatigue emerged from a deeper level. Sitting in Wang Liping's energy field engages with the self on the level of our *shen*, especially if we are able to stabilize our mind and body while enduring the pressure.

In Korea, I kept working to stabilize my *xiatian*. I would tune into the internal pulsing and allow it to unfold. The trick was stillness; my body and mind had to be extraordinarily quiet. I found breathing to be the greatest obstacle. Although the inside of my body was full of noises, breathing was by far the loudest. I regulated my breath to be as quiet as possible and eventually reached a point where I did not even want to breathe. I knew that as soon as I inhaled, I could potentially lose track of the energetic pulse—a kind of energy called *jing*. At first it can be very slippery to grasp. Working with it involves sifting through layers of noise in search of a distant signal.

Partway through the intensive, Wang Liping introduced us to what he called "the self with form but no substance" (*youxing wuzhe de wo* 有形物質的我). Also known as the subtle body, it feels like an energetic field following the contours of the physical body. Working with it led to one of the most powerful experiences of my life. Near the end of one session, the pulsing of my *xiatian* opened up and my body filled with *qi*. The more I tuned into the movement of the *xiatian*, the more this *qi* permeated my body. It was thick and bright, and it infused my head, chest, abdomen, and limbs, pulsing in time with my *xiatian*. After a few moments, I lost all sense of my physical body. All the discomfort and noise of my body completely disappeared. Time stood still. All I could feel was my energy body and the hum of my *xiatian*.

Later, while resting in my room, it occurred to me that I was in an altered state. I felt as though I was looking at things from some sort of ultimate perspective. I understood everything. For the next twenty-four hours, everything connected to the human experience just made sense. All the stress and anxiety of being me evaporated. My ego-self was gone. I just existed. This experience was accompanied with a feeling of complete contentment. Then, little by little, I came back into my physical body and returned to normal. I lost connection with this vast field of understanding. I also understood on a deeper level how uncomfortable the physical body can be. No wonder babies cry so much, where they must transition from spirit to the confined quarters of living in the body. This profound experience left me with a clearer sense of how we are much more than just our physical bodies and conceptual minds. Helping others experience this is what motivates me to teach Wang Liping's lineage of Taoism.

Winter 2014/15

After my third intensive, I felt like I was starting to gain some real traction with my training. Even though I still had a lot left to learn, I finally started to feel more confident. I returned to Vancouver and trained with this newly found motivation.

Although I focused on the *neidan* techniques I had learned from Wang Liping, I also kept up my Wu family tai chi and *neigong* practice, which helped immensely with my study of *neidan*. As strange as it may sound, I even started learning methods in dreams. On several different occasions, I learned a specific *neidan* technique while asleep. The hardest thing to grasp when learning *neidan* is the correct feeling; in fact, the main job of a *neidan* teacher is trying to get students to feel what the teacher feels while practicing. Dreams allow us to experience the correct feeling, and if we can remember it when we wake, we can integrate it into our practice. This is my favourite dream technique, and I still use it regularly.

The first method that I learned in my dreams elevated my practice to a new level. The technique involved combining a certain feeling with specific breathing techniques, along with the intention to raise the vibration of the physical body to that of light. When I finally put it to the test, I released a large amount of *qi*. The first thing I noticed was a shift in my hearing, as though I had suddenly placed myself in a vacuum or donned noise-cancelling headphones. Surge after surge of *qi* went through my system. This was accompanied by a bright light, which seemed to increase with every rush of *qi*. After things subsided, I felt a new rhythm in my body: a ten-second, wave-like sensation. It was both a feeling and a sound; the soundscape of my inner body brightened and darkened in time with this oscillation.

The whole experience was very calming and soothing. It went on for about five minutes and was accompanied by an emotional release that cleaned out some blocked *qi* from my left leg. Afterward, my body felt clean, fresh, and energetically elevated—so much so that I continue to use this technique regularly. It seems to work best when sitting in full lotus cross-legged position, which allows me to amass a fair bit of *qi*. It also dovetails nicely with other practices Wang Liping taught me years later, ones that work directly with the light body (*shenguang zhi shen* 神光之身).

In another dream, someone began pressing on my head with some sort of tool. I felt a pressing sensation slowly work its way up the back of my head. When it reached the crown, it became increasingly intense, as if made by chopsticks. It was a little scary, but it also felt quite enjoyable. After I woke up, the *baihui* acupoint at the top of my head buzzed for several hours.

During this time, I also experimented with techniques from books, limiting myself primarily to variations on techniques I had already learned. Wang Liping's *The Blue Book* particularly helped. While reading through it, I stumbled upon a method of working with True *Jing*, a form of *qi* in our bodies. The results were impressive. Sitting in full lotus, I sealed off the Seven Upper Openings and the Upper Space with nose breathing. Then I dropped my awareness down to my Lower Space while keeping *qi* in the Upper Space. I ever so gently contracted my lower belly with the inhale. Wang Liping writes that if you do this correctly, you can feel a small drop of something—our True *Jing*—begin to descend along a certain pathway. I could feel something falling like a little raindrop. I guided it to my *xiatian*. There was a rush of vibration, heat, and light. It felt fantastic! I was so excited that I could only maintain it in my *xiatian* for a few seconds. But I learnt something important: full lotus gets results, while giddy excitement curbs them.

The biggest obstacle to my training has always been my health. I was never gifted with a robust constitution; when I was young, I often contracted severe colds, flus, and migraine headaches. Although my health improved after I started training with Wang Liping, my kidneys remained weak. In Chinese medical theory, kidneys are responsible for regulating our *jing* energy. I had classic kidney *yin* deficiency. I had frequent cold sweats at night, and I had to severely limit sexual activity in order not to exhaust myself.

During the spring of 2015, I actually stopped sexual activity of any kind. This decision naturally arose out of my practice. I just knew that sex was not what my body needed. My wife was once again very understanding and supportive. This self-imposed abstinence lasted nine months; now my kidneys are strong, and I have an abundance of *jing*.

Korea, April 2015

In April 2015, I flew to Korea for another intensive with Wang Liping. I felt more prepared this time because I was regularly sitting for two hours at a stretch, my hips were open, and my legs were at ease. This was something I could only dream about a year ago. I was much less intimidated by the prospect of the bitter training. Taoist alchemy is fun, but it can also be quite difficult, requiring a certain level of commitment and resolve.

This time around, Wang Liping focused on the *xiatian*. I spent each session focused inside my lower abdominal cavity, listening to it hum while my body pulsed with *jing* energy. Wang Liping explains that where there is movement, or vibration, there is also sound. He teaches a technique called Inner Hearing to tune into the movement of *qi* inside the body. What we tune into is both a movement and a sound—a concept that can really open up our practice.

After a few days, I began to hear something new: a rising and falling tone embedded within the hum of my *xiatian*. It had a consistent tone and oscillated about once per second, slower than the field itself. Eventually it became clear that the *xiatian* hummed because it was turning very fast, and the new tone resulted from this spinning. The *xiatian* was turning inside the lower abdominal cavity around an axis between my hips. The direction of the spin was upwards at the back and downwards in front. The spinning was creating an overtone of sorts. If you have ever listened to a fan turn very fast, you may have heard a slower brightening and darkening tone embedded within the sound of the hum. That is the sound I kept hearing. As I tuned into this spinning sensation, the lower half of my torso, from perineum to solar plexus, became very hot and started to sweat.

Over the next few days, the movement in my *xiatian* began to activate other areas of my body. It brightened the inside of my torso with its comfortable, soothing movement. It rocked my spine back and forth with a gentle, wave-like sensation. It even prompted the *qi* that filled my head cavity to rotate in time with its slow oscillation.

For the remainder of the intensive, *qi* continued to flood my body. Wang Liping was teaching us to work with the non-physical body and expanding the hum of my *xiatian* past my physical body into my non-physical body helped greatly. The main channel of *qi* that runs down the front of my body opened up as well. My whole body felt like a pulsing mass of *qi*.

Southeast Asia, July 2015

It was good to be back in Southeast Asia. The first few days of my visit were pleasant. I hung out for a few days and caught up with old friends. But when I joined the intensive, my *xiatian* almost immediately started pulsing. Southeast Asia 2015 was another twenty-one-day fasting retreat, and as such it was considerably more demanding than my previous intensive. While in Korea, I felt like I was surfing on top of the wave. But in Southeast Asia, I felt like the wave had crashed over me, pulled me under, and ripped me apart. In those days, the Southeast Asian group would regularly sit for over three hours at a stretch during their fasting retreats. Admittedly, it worked. I felt the results.

I started sitting on a wood board during this particular intensive. This method of sitting concentrates the weight of the body directly onto the sit bones rather than spreading it evenly over the legs. The sit bones begin to burn. If we are able to hold our position long enough, our *qi* begins to transform, opening up energy meridians in the body. Once the sit bones open, in the future they will generally not burn again, no matter how long we sit.

For me, Southeast Asia 2015 revolved around past lives. While practicing, I witnessed scenes and associated drama from several different, sometimes interconnected past lives. At a certain point in our training, practitioners work through the reincarnation energy (*zhuanshi nengliang* 轉世能量) stored inside the body. This usually happens when we start working on the *zhongtian* (Middle Field). Wang Liping disclosed that it took him several years to go through the process. A practitioner who has completely reconciled their past, including their past lives, is called a *zhenren* 真人 or perfected person. Over the course of twenty-one days, I went through seven or eight lives. The content was always negative, consisting of material that I had not been able or willing to process before then. Another practitioner on the same retreat went through over 20 lives.

In Southeast Asia, I began to explore another odd aspect of Taoist training called working with the Hidden Teacher (*mingshi* 冥師). On a rudimentary level, the Hidden Teacher can be understood as a personification of our intuitive, all-knowing self. This teacher exists somewhere inside our body, and it is up to us to find and make contact. There is a Taoist saying that "to bring our *shen* into our body, we make an offering of *jing* and *qi*; but to find our hidden teacher, we offer solitude and quiet." In the past, Taoist initiates would undertake a solitary retreat for this purpose. During the Southeast Asian retreat, I made contact with my Hidden Teacher, only to lose it when I started thinking too much. The Hidden Teacher gives us information about our practice and even our life, but this guidance stops coming if we doubt or overanalyze it. At higher levels of practice, our Hidden Teacher's counsel is essential, even trumping that of our flesh and blood teacher.

Over the course of the intensive, my *xiatian* continued to activate and my *shenguang* became increasingly luminous. Wang Liping introduced a specific method for activating the *xiatian* that involved harnessing *jing* from the kidneys. The retreat was tough; I was exhausted and my body ached. There were times I could not imagine going on, but somehow I made it through. On the last session, I experienced a humming, warm, bright ball of *qi* in my Lower Space. This consolation from a difficult retreat sent me home on a high.

Korea, November 2015

In November, I travelled to Korea for another intensive with Wang Liping. By now I was starting to feel more comfortable with the practice. This was my third time with the Korean group, and I was glad to be back. Over the course of ten days, the group worked to form the elixir. The elixir, one of the goals of *neidan*, is a super-charged ball of energy. It can be formed in a variety of ways, but one of the more dynamic of these is the Nine Times Firing Process (see future volumes).

As the days progressed, the activation of my *xiatian* became more and more intense. I also began to feel more at home within my lower abdominal cavity. When I began a session and started to do the work, I felt as though my perspective had dropped down inside my torso. This phenomenon has only increased as my practice has deepened.

Over the course of the training, the intensity of my *xiatian* continued to increase and I began to see images. One night, while working on sleep practice, my *xiatian* became bright and started to pulse, heating my whole body but especially my lumbar spine. I saw a number of abstract geometric symbols, including a mandala, deep inside my lower abdomen. After I finished the practice, I went to sleep. That night I had a dream that I was inside a round, damp cavern with a white spider. The cavern was the same shape as my lower abdominal cavity. In the dream I was trying to light a wick the height of my *xiatian* that grew from the cavern floor, but the spider would not let me ignite it. To form the elixir, we need to purge any turbid *qi* we have in our torso. From this dream, I gathered that there was still some purging to do.

On the seventh day, we started the Nine Times Firing Process, an intense practice that synchronizes the expansion and contraction of the lower belly, genitals, anus, and kidneys with the extension of the spine. On retreat it is performed nine times per session and undertaken in nine consecutive sessions stretched out over a few days. The first time I tried it, my *xiatian* heated up significantly and I felt something substantial and almost spherical inside. Near the end of the session, when we were sitting quietly, my Microcosmic Orbit started to open. Unfortunately, the session ended before it could fully activate. Everyone in the group was pretty excited after the session. This was, for most of us, our first experience with the Firing Process. I felt hot and tired, as well as experiencing aches in my body, for the remainder of the day. Even while lying down, my *xiatian* just kept cooking. I was also developing a host of physical side-effects including sore teeth and gums, a buildup of earwax, and dry mucous in my eyes and nose.

Over the next few days, we kept working on the Firing Process, supplementing this with a generous amount of silent sitting. On the ninth day, when I went through the firing process, I was unable to amass the same amount of heat. My furnace had cooled. This happens when the lower abdominal cavity has not been properly sealed. I had managed to collect the ingredients and put them in the cauldron, but when I cooked them, they could not catch fire.

Regardless, the session was amazing. During the silent sitting, a column of light wrapped around my spine, extending from my tailbone to the top of the head and down the front to my celestial eye point. The column was approximately two inches in diameter and ran perfectly straight, disregarding the curves of my spine. A faint trace of *qi* continued down the front of my body, running from between my eyebrows to my perineum. As I sat, my middle field opened up in my chest, full and bright. I saw an image of my parents in my lower abdomen, and there, encompassing it, was the sphere I had seen on the seventh day when I started the firing process. It was not fully formed, but it did feel three-dimensional. It reminded me of a waxing moon, three-quarters full.

Winter 2015/16

After my return to Vancouver, I continued to train. My practice had begun to develop significant momentum, so much so that I completed up to three sessions a day. I usually started the day with a lengthy *neidan* session, which generally took place between 3:00 and 6:00 in the morning. In the afternoon, I incorporated standing postures, Wu family *neigong*, and other internal martial art practices. I usually concluded the day's activities with a shorter silent session in full-lotus posture.

During this time, I began seeing the spiritual illumination of the *shenguang* more frequently, which led in turn to many strange and unusual experiences. Early one morning, for example, while following the opening steps of the Celestial Eye practice, I entered a focused stillness. The silence was so great that I ceased breathing. After a few moments, my Inner Vision spontaneously shifted in a manner similar to what happens when redirecting one's gaze to the horizon. This occurred in tandem with a trembling sensation and a rush of *qi* and light. Once these feelings stabilized, I saw a small pool of light rotating around a central hole of pure blackness. This was followed, while sitting in stillness, by a sheet of white mist. After the session, I began to receive a lot of information, so I sat down in front of the fireplace to process everything. I eventually decided to go back to sleep, but as soon as I closed my eyes, I saw many images. I had such a profound dream that night that I could not recall it in my conscious state.

Perhaps the greatest impression from this period was the recognition that the practice has a life of its own. There is an odd balancing act between working toward a goal and allowing a process to unfold of its own accord. For example, one day the energy channel running down the front of my body opened up. Even though I was not specifically working on the channel, it opened. As in Korea, it manifested as a thick straight column of *qi* that reached from my forehead to my genitals during silent sitting. Within the column of *qi* was a strong downward current. It felt wonderful.

When I reread my practice journal, I was struck by how perfectly these experiences dovetailed together. Two weeks previously, the area at the back of my head known as the jade pillow had energetically opened, without any conscious effort on my part. Even through the crown of my head had been opening gradually over the previous year, the jade pillow area had remained blocked. Once it opened, I could feel a painful process of the *qi* beginning to circulate up the back of my head and across my crown. This phenomenon was followed, a week later, by the opening of the internal centreline in my torso, from my heart down to my perineum, and then the energy channel running down the front of my body. In most cases, with the exception of the internal centreline, this is a classic Taoist alchemy sequence known as the Microcosmic Orbit.

Although this orbit had opened a couple years earlier in Southeast Asia, it was now opening with a different kind of energy. As in Southeast Asia, I had never intended to open it; rather, the orbit launched on its own accord while doing silent sitting. These events served to remind me that we cannot think our way through the process. Wisdom comes in knowing when to do something and when to let things be.

China, March 2016

In March, I joined an intensive in Dalian, China, with the Korean group and a number of Chinese students. The focus of the retreat was the continuation of the Firing Process, which Wang Liping had introduced the previous November. I felt ready this time. The Firing Process requires lengthy sits of at least two and a half hours each, and my sits were consistently over the two-hour mark. It also helps to have the Inner Cavity and Three Spaces work out of the way before attempting the practice, and I had taken care of this back in Austria. I was ready to go.

Three days into the intensive, during a long silent sitting session, my Microcosmic Orbit opened up again. This time, a small sphere of *qi*, about the size of a grape, quickly ran through the circuit five or six times. It dropped from my *xiatian* to my perineum, sped up my spine and over my head, and ran down the front of my torso before returning to the perineum. Each cycle lasted about a second. Once the ball of *qi* returned to my *xiatian*, I felt faint and my hands were cold and clammy. I was extremely cold after the session and started to shiver uncontrollably. My teeth were chattering with such intensity that I could not even talk. My Korean friends helped me back to my room, covered me with blankets, and nursed me with hot tea. A few hours later, my spine started to feel sore, as if it had been physically manipulated. I remained cold all night. I tried tea, hot showers, and warm clothes, but nothing seemed to help. The only thing that made a difference was the usual morning walking practice. As I walked, I focused on bringing *qi* down the internal centreline of my torso. Fortunately, I immediately warmed up once I moved the *qi* into my *xiatian* and started breathing with my lower abdomen.

The next day, Wang Liping told me not to worry. He explained that there were different substances that could go through the Microcosmic Orbit. I experienced what is known as the liquid form of the elixir, and it cooled when returning to the *xiatian*. For the rest of the intensive, we continued to work on the Firing Process, but I kept running up against the limits of my physical body. To form the elixir, the physical body needs to be conditioned; it must be both supple, like a baby's body, and structurally sound. Even after years of practicing internal martial arts, I was not strong enough.

Think of it this way: When we are sitting still for two to three hours at a time, our torso can begin to shift or even collapse. In my case, my chest began to cave in, which in turn compromised the structural integrity of my inner space. To form the elixir, we need to maintain the space where it is formed for long periods of time, simultaneously managing the energetic pressure and holding our awareness inside the body. During each session, I would follow the instructions and achieve promising results, but throughout the final hour of silent sitting, known as Bathing and Cleansing, the elixir would fail to crystallize. I was just not able to hold everything together sufficiently. But during a silent session the day after the retreat, I could feel a heavy spherical weight inside my lower abdominal cavity. The weight eventually disappeared after a few days. I was so close!

Teaching

On the last day of the 2015 Southeast Asia intensive, Wang Liping told me to start teaching Taoist alchemy. He recommended that I avoid workshops or retreats for a while in lieu of weekly classes. I felt a little intimidated by the thought of teaching, but Wang Liping was very encouraging. Keep it simple and teach what you know, he said.

By autumn 2015, I had put together a website, prepared a curriculum, and rented classroom space in Vancouver's Chinatown. I set the start date for the following April, a month after the Dalian intensive. I remember the first course fondly. Five students showed up hungry to learn. They were a fun crew.

Energetic transmission is an important part of Wang Liping's *neidan* and figuring out how to regulate the energy field in a room (*tiao qichang* 調氣場) was especially fun. Wang Liping gave me a general overview of the method and Quan Guanhua filled in a few more details. The process was, I later realized, actually just an application of certain techniques I had already learned, so I decided to give it a try.

Regulating the field needs a considerable amount of energetic juice, and I was not sure if my students would feel it, so I really went for it. I tuned into the movement of *qi* in my Inner Cavity and expanded it into the practice space, setting up a resonance with the *qi* field in the room. Then I adjusted the field according to Wang Liping's instructions. Everything seemed to go well, and after the session I was excited to note that a few of the students had consciously felt the field. Interesting, I thought, it worked. Then I went home and basically slept for a week. Regulating the field had exhausted me, especially since I had really applied myself in the process.

Helping students individually took time to figure out. Wang Liping explained that we all possess not only a unique age, sex, and cultural background, but also a distinctive learning style. Additionally, we are often restricted in our practice by issues like *qi* blockages, unresolved trauma, and karmic heritage, which all have profound influence on our life and practice. To further complicate matters, we are often not even aware of these issues; instead, we tiptoe around them our entire lives, blind to their existence.

Wang Liping encouraged me to figure out what each student needed and to help them along their journey by adapting the material to their circumstances. He recommended that as students were working through issues, that I note to myself, the steps I had taken to address these issues, and the outcome.

While leading *neidan* sessions, I began to open up to information in a new way. As I extended my *qi* field over a group, I began to receive bits of information in the form of images, feelings, and words that I knew were not mine. Because this new ability was still in its infancy, I found it difficult to match the information I received with a specific student. I found it even more challenging, however, to communicate this information in a helpful way. Wang Liping advised caution: "help," he told me, "is not always helpful." Sometimes we need to struggle with an issue for a while before we can allow ourselves to move on. Wang Liping often uses humour and other roundabout ways to make a point. He also avoids belabouring an issue or offering the same advice twice. He leaves it up to you to accept or reject his counsel as you see fit.

During *neidan* sessions, I was sometimes able to help students move their blocked *qi*. This would happen spontaneously and I had no control over the process. While leading students, I would sense an emotion or image and start to tremble. Sometimes a student would cry out or have some sort of reaction, and other times I would notice someone quietly crying or looking out of sorts after the session. In the early days, these experiences would leave me feeling drained and I would often develop a cough or a scratchy throat. Sometimes I would even have more severe symptoms, such as headaches or diarrhea. I would usually need to sit for full personal *neidan* session just to normalize. When I asked Wang Liping about this, he just laughed. "Teaching this stuff is not easy," he said. It was not until I started teaching that I grasped how much Wang Liping puts into his intensives and his students.

Practicing Taoist alchemy has opened my eyes to a whole new world of experiences connected with my energy body. After years of qigong and neigong training, I thought I had really experienced *qi*. *Neidan* is different. Strange new energetic phenomena arise in my body on a routine basis. I continue to practice daily and train with Wang Liping regularly. I am currently attempting to form the Sacred Embryo, an absolutely fascinating process of self-transformation. I hope this account has been of interest. May your own personal journey be just as rewarding.

Epilogue

The path of Taoist cultivation is long. There is always more to learn. Once we think we understand, we do not understand. Keep going. The same can be said of this book. It is not the truth. It is just my understanding based on my present perspective. Hopefully my perspective will continue to evolve. Taoist alchemy is massive. It is an all-encompassing practice. Who we think we are changes over time. Our life changes as we surrender to the *qi*. There is always more. As Chapter One of the *Daode Jing* states, "Profound mystery upon profound mystery until we penetrate to the gateway of the marvelous." In other words, keep it going.

玄之又玄, 眾妙之門.

Appendices

Appendix 1: Overview of the Dragon Gate System

In this portion, you will find an overview of Wang Liping's Dragon Gate system of Taoist training: The Internal Art of Penetrating to the Numinous Treasure and Wisdom Ability (*Lingbaotong zhineng neigong shu* 靈寶通智能內功術).

Wang Liping teaches internal alchemy (*neidan*) and the Taoist Five Arts (fate calculation, appearance discernment, divination, practices, and medicine). *Neidan* powers the Five Arts. The core of Wang Liping's teaching contains three components:

1. Yinxian Methods (silent sitting)
2. Three Immortals Practice (*neidan*)
3. Celestial Eye Practice

The practices in this book are mostly drawn from the Yinxian Methods and a little bit from the Three Immortals Practice.

Yinxian Methods (silent sitting)

Yinxian Methods (*Yinxian fa* 引仙法) are the way of silent sitting used in the Dragon Gate Lineage and they form an essential platform for the practice of *neidan*. Before we can practice *neidan*, we need to prepare. The 12 methods are a collection of techniques and principles used throughout the alchemical process to regulate the mind and body and enter stillness.

    i   Gather the Mind and Sit Quietly

    ii   Regulate the Body

    iii No Seeing, No Hearing

    iv Gather in the Vision and Return the Hearing

    v   Regulate Normal Breathing

    vi The Three Step Practice of Calming, Creating, and Gathering In the Spirit

    vii Regulate the True Breath

    viii Sealing up the Body

    ix Inner Vision and Return the Hearing

    x   Concentrate the Spirit and Begin Quiet Illumination

    xi Listen and Follow the Breath

    xii Nourish the Heart to Bath and Cleanse

The first three methods are the core of the practice, and the remaining nine are supplemental. The methods are not meant to be followed sequentially. Apply them as needed.

Methods One to Seven are for restoring us to our original healthy state.
Methods Eight to Nine are for repairing energetic leakages in the body.
Methods Ten to Twelve are for building foundation.

Three Immortals Practice (Internal Alchemy, *Neidan*)

To transform the self, we follow the way of alchemy. Internal alchemy (*neidan* 內丹) is a form of esoteric Taoist meditation that works with our body and its energies. It seeks to refine and change coarser energetic states into more rarified states. Just as ice turns to water, and water turns to steam, the self can also be transformed. It is often seen as the pinnacle of Taoist self-transformation practices and is often passed on privately between teacher and student.

The training has five stages:

1. Refining the body to conserve the *qi* (foundation practice)

2. Refining essence into *qi*

3. Refining *qi* into spirit

4. Refining spirit to revert to emptiness

5. Refining emptiness to join with the Tao

The order of the methods below is not carved in stone; they only describe a general trajectory. All the parts work together as an organic whole. Master Wang advises us not to plot our practice, but instead use our intuition and approach the process in a state of *wuwei*.

Three Immortals Practice (*sanxian gong* 三仙功) is the main body of the alchemical work. It is the private oral teaching associated with Lü Dongbin's alchemical classic *Lingbao bifa*. Three Immortals Practice is divided into three vehicles, ten gates, and 45 methods.

The Practice of Human Transcendence

Furnace is the body. Medicine is *qi*. Fire is the heart. Water is the kidneys. Cultivates Life Force (*minggong* 命功).

1. Pairing of Yin and Yang
  i   The *Yang* Embryo and the *Yin* Breath
  ii True Embryo Breathing
  iii Pairing of *Kan* and *Li*

2. Gathering and Dispersing the Water and Fire
  i   The True *Qi* Contained in the Original Union of *Yin* and *Yang*
  ii The Lesser Refining of the Form
  iii Celestial Youth

3. Copulation of the Dragon and Tiger
  i   Gather and Nourish the Reverted Elixir
  ii Foster the Transcendent Embryo
  iii Water and Fire, *Kan* and Li
  iv The True Husband and Wife
  v   Exchange the *Qi*, not the Form

4. Refine the Medicine for the Elixir
  i   Fire Phasing
  ii Lesser Celestial Circuit
  iii Fire Phasing for the Celestial Circuit

    iv Gather the Spirit to Nourish the *Qi*

    v Gather the *Qi* to Nourish the Spirit

    vi Refine the *Yang* to Nourish the Spirit

The Practice of Earthly Transcendence

Furnace is spirit. Medicine is *qi.* Fire is the sun. Water is the moon. Cultivates Life Force (*minggong* 命功).

5. Flying the Golden Crystals Behind the Elbows

    i Revert Essence to Nourish the Brain

    ii Initiate the River Chariot

    iii Copulation of the Dragon and Tiger

    iv Decrease Lead Increase Mercury

    v Revert to Youth from Old Age

6. Reverted Elixir of Jade Liquid

    i Jade Liquid Refines the Talisman

    ii Bathing and Cleansing the Transcendent Embryo

    iii The Lesser Reverted Elixir

    iv The Greater Reverted Elixir

    v The Seven-Returned Elixir

    vi The Nine-Revolved Elixir

7. Reverted Elixir of Golden Liquid

    i Golden Elixir Refines the Talismanic Form

    ii Ignite the Alchemic Flame Setting the Body on Fire

    iii The Golden Flower and the Jade Dew

    iv Greater *Kan* and Li

    v The Method of Yellow and White

The Practice of Celestial Transcendence

Furnace is spirit. Medicine is inner nature. Fire is wisdom. Water is stability. Cultivates Inner Nature (*xinggong* 性功).

8. Refine *Qi* to have an Audience with the Origin

    i   Transcend the Inner Courtyard

    ii Refine *Qi* to Complete the Form

    iii The Purple and Golden Elixir

    iv Scorch and Refine the *Yang* Spirit

    v   The Three Blossomings Accumulate on the Top of the Head

9. Inner Observation of the Exchange

    i   Collect the *Yang* Spirit

    ii Fire that Reaches to Heaven

    iii Exchange the Ordinary with the Transcendent

    iv True Emptiness

    v   Entering the Celestial Kingdom

10. Liberation from Form

    i   Enter the Formless

    ii Cast Off the Material and Transcend

    iii Transcend the Ordinary and Enter the Sacred

Celestial Eye Practice

Celestial Eye Practice is the oral teaching associated with the text *The Secret of the Golden Flower*, and is used in all stages of training alongside Three Immortals Practice. This practice opens the Celestial Eye (Third Eye) and works with the Light of our Spirit (*shenguang* 神光). It also cultivates our Inner Nature (*xinggong* 性功).

There are ten stages with four methods each, but Wang Liping has only taught the first four stages publicly.

1. Open Celestial Eye

    i   Use Awareness to Transport the Spiritual Illumination

    ii Open the Celestial Eye

    iii Exchange of *Kan* and *Li*

    iv Three Lights Gather Naturally

2. Ancestral Opening Practice

  i   Return the Light and Collect the *Ling*

  ii   Rotate the Sun and Moon

  iii   Unite the Sun and Moon

  iv   *Ling* Accumulates in the Mysterious Opening

3. Concentrate *Shen* in *Xiatian*

  i   Close your Eyes and Return the Light

  ii   Manufacture the Medicine in the Palace of Earth

  iii   Regulate the Breath to Bathe and Cleanse

  iv   Gather the Light into a Small Pearl

4. Turn Around Observation and Illuminate Interior

  i   Spirit Leads the Small Pearl

  ii   Transport and Transform the Five Phases

  iii   Spirit and *Ling* Become One

  iv   Gently Nourish the Dragon's Pearl

Supplemental Practices

The three practices above are core (Yinxian Methods, Three Immortals Practice, Celestial Eye Practice). The following are supplemental.

1. Female Alchemy
2. Seven Star Stepping, Nine Palace Bagua Stepping, Bagua Intention Sphere, and the Three Methods of Opening the Energy Channels, Meridians, and Channels in the Bones
3. Method for Stealing the Essence of the Sun and Moon to Return to the Self
4. Energy Balancing Practice (tree practice) and Standing Meditation Practice
5. The Nature Energy Exchange Method (Taoist Walking)
6. Paired Practice

Appendix 2: Glossary

Taoist Alchemy Terms

The glossary includes the Chinese terms from this book and other terms useful for *neidan* practice.

ān lú shè dǐng 安爐設鼎 – stabilize the furnace and set up the cauldron

Bǎihuì 百會 – highest area in the physical body. Highest point on top of the head. To find, draw two lines straight up from the ears to the top of the head.

Bāguà zhang 八卦掌 – Eight Trigram Palm, an internal martial art.

Chén 沉 – to sink.

Chū shén 出神 – the *shen* intentionally exits the body. *Shen chu* 神出 means the *shen* has unintentionally been scattered outside the body. Practitioners want the first one, not the second.

Dào 道 – literally means "way".

Dàojiào 道教 – Taoism.

Dàojiā 道家 – Taoism.

Dǎoyǐn 導引 – the traditional term for Chinese health and *qi* exercises.

Dǎoyǐn cí 導引詞 – guided instructions.

Dǎoyǐn shù 導引術 – the art of using guided instructions. Dragon Gate alchemy is passed on using *daoyin shu*.

Gǎnwù 感悟 – to sense, but not through our physical senses.

Gōng 功 – practice (n); the acquired development of embodied skill.
- *gōngfu* 功夫 – kungfu, but really any high level of embodied skill developed through practice

Hòutiān 後天 – Postcelestial, later heaven, after creation of phenomenal world; postnatal (Chinese med.)

Hǔohòu 火候 – Fire Phasing; this is a cooking term that describes how much heat is needed to cook something. In alchemy it refers to how strong to make our intention, *shen*, and our breath in order to cook the elixir.
- Wénhǔo 文火 – Civil Fire; gentle fire phasing
- Wǔhǔo 武火 – Martial Fire; strong fire phasing
- Wénwǔhǔo 文武火 – breath starts gentle and increases in strength
- Wǔwénhǔo 武文火 – breath starts strong and becomes gentle

Huángtíng 黃庭 – the Yellow Court. Describes a central area used when bringing together *yin* and *yang* during the alchemical process. The term does not refer to a single location; it changes depending on what we are doing.

Huǐguò 悔過 – repentance training. Used to purify turbid *qi*.

Huìyīn 會陰 – Lowest area in the torso, between the anus and genitals. One of the Three Lower Yin Gates.
- Huìyīn xué 會陰穴 – The acupoint in the middle of the *Huiyin*.

Hūxi 呼吸 – breathing.
- Zìran hūxi 自然呼吸 – Natural Breathing. Also called normal breath *fanxi* 凡息, the opposite of True Breath (*zhenxi* 真息). There is regulated and unregulated.
- Nèixíng hūxi 內行呼吸 – Inner Breathing. Breathing that is focused inside the body.
- Máokǒng hūxi 毛孔呼吸 – Pore Breathing. Called Personal Universe Breathing (*zishen yuzhou huxi* 自身宇宙呼吸) in the old days.
- Sǎnhǔo hūxi 散火呼吸 – Disperse Fire Breathing. Used to close a session.

Jiādào 家道 – a temple lineage of Taoist practice. Contrast with *Shandao*.

Jīběn gōng 基本功 – foundation training.

Jiédān 結丹 – form an Elixir.

Jìn 劲 – a specific force developed and used in martial arts training.

Jīng 精 – the energy of our physical essence; *jing – qi – shen* (the Three Treasures of the body); a kind of lower frequency energy found in the body, which through *neidan* practice is transformed into higher frequency energy. This is the alchemical ingredient used for forming elixirs in the Lower Dantian.

Jīngqì 精氣 – *jing* and *qi* together. This term is used when working with *jing* and *qi* together. Often used with lower level alchemy techniques.

Jìng 靜 – stillness (foundation of Taoist practice)
* **jìnggōng** 靜功 – stillness practice
* **lìan jìng** 練靜 – practice stillness

Kōng 空 – empty
* **fàngkōng** 放空 – to empty, to make something empty

Kuà 胯 – the *kua* includes all the tendons and muscles that run through the groin area (inguinal crease). We have a *kua* on both left and right sides.

Kūngōng 坤宫 – Palace of Kun (Earth); Another of the many terms for the *xiatian* (Lower Dantian)

Líng 靈 – spirit; our eternal spirit that merges with our *shen* at conception (*shen* is the spirit of our body). *Ling* exists before and after our physical body's existence.

Liùhébāfǎ 六合八法 – a rare internal martial art. Literally Six Harmonies and Eight Methods, also known as water boxing.

Líupài 流派 – Lineages.

Mǎoyǒu zhōutiān 卯酉周天 – the Maoyou Cosmic Orbit. The energy circuit throughout our internal organs.

Mìnggōng 命功 – Life Force Practice. Works with the more material aspects of the self, such as the physical body, *jing* and *qi*. Usually works with the Lower and Middle Fields. Contrast with *Xinggong*.

Míngqiào 明竅 – sense organs in the head.

Míngshī 冥師 – our Hidden Teacher, found inside our body.

Mùyù 沐浴 – bathing and cleansing. An important stage in forming the Elixir and the Embryo.

Nèidān 內丹 – internal alchemy (literally internal cinnabar). Other words for internal alchemy:

- **lian dān** 煉丹 – practice alchemy (literally refine the elixir)
- **dāndào** 丹道 – Way of Alchemy
- **jīndān** 金丹 – Golden Elixir
- **jīndān zhī dào** 金丹之道 – Way of the Golden Elixir

Nèigōng 內功 – internal work or internal art (a broad term used to encapsulate a wide variety of internal practices, generally not a specific practice).

Nèiqì 內炁 – inner *qi*. Stuff we create in our body.

Nèiqiāng 內腔 – Inner Cavity. When the abdominal cavity, chest cavity, and head cavity are sealed and connected they form the Inner Cavity. The Inner Cavity is an internal energetic space used for advanced alchemical practices.

Nèiyào 內藥 – literally Internal Medicine. I translate this as Internal Alchemical Ingredients. Also called the Small Pill.

Nìwǎn 泥丸 – Muddy Pellet. Another term for the Upper Field.

- *Niwan gong* 泥丸宮 – Palace of the Muddy Pellet. Another term for the Upper Field.

Nèizhào 內照 – inner illumination.

Rùyào 入藥 – depositing the Alchemical Ingredients into the cauldron.

Sānbāo 三寶 – The Three Treasures:

- Internal Three Treasures are *jing*, *qi*, and *shen* energy.
- External Three Treasures are sun, moon, and stars

Sānkōng 三空 – The Three Spaces

- Internal Three Spaces: 1. lower abdominal cavity 2. chest cavity 3. head cavity
- External Three Spaces: 1. personal space (arms length from body) 2. social space (human society) 3. natural cosmic space

Sān tiān 三田 – the Three Fields: *shangtian*, *zhongtian*, and *xiatian*.

Sān xià yīn 三下陰 – The Lower Three Yin Gates. These need to be energetically sealed during the alchemical process.

- **Qiányīn** 前陰 – (literally Front Yin) where the genitals attach to the torso.
- **Huìyīn** 會陰 – Bottom of the torso, between the anus and genitals (perineum).
- **Hòuyīn** 後陰 – Anus. Also known as the Lower Magpie Bridge.

Sānxiān Gōng 三仙功 – Three Immortals Practice. The *neidan* curriculum of the Dragon Gate Lineage.

Shāndào 山道 – Mountain lineage of Taoist practice. Contrast with *Jiadao*.

Shàngtiān 上田 – the Upper Field, commonly referred to as the Upper Dantian. This energy centre is in the middle of the head on the level of the eyebrows, usually just behind the temples.

Shàng Qī Míngqiào 上七明竅 – The Upper Seven Openings. Two eyes, two ears, two nostrils, and one mouth. Places where our *shishen* easily leaks out. Need to be sealed.

Shén 神 – spirit. The high frequency energy of conscious awareness.
- **yúanshén** 元神 – original spirit; our precelestial *shen*; it's found inside our body and good to get to know. *Yuanshen* splits into *yin shen* and *yang shen*. It is also master of our *shishen*.
- **shíshén** 識神 – (literally spirit of recognition); our postcelestial *shen*, given birth through our senses, gives birth to the seven feelings; our ego this-world self.

Shéngōng 神功 – practice that works with our *shen* or spirit, common in *neidan* practice.

Shéngūang 神光 – light of our spirit; spiritual illumination; it's also wisdom and a good way to work with our nature (*xing* 性).

Shénguāng zhī shēn 神光之身 – the light body.

Shénlèi 神累 – tired spirit. Happens after too much *shen* work.

Shèngtāi 聖胎 – sacred embryo.

Shēnfǎ 身法 – literally body method. The specific manner of using the body in martial art training.

Shénqì 神氣 – spirit and *qi* together, often used in mid-level alchemy techniques.

Shényì 神意 – spirit and intention together, often used in higher level alchemy techniques.

Shì 視 – to see.
i. **yuǎn shí** 遠視 – To See Afar
ii. **fǎn guān** 反觀 – To Turn Around Observation
iii. **nèi shí** 內視 – Inner Seeing
iv. **nèi guān** 內觀 – Inner Observation

Shī chuán 失傳 – lost transmission.

Shuìgōng 睡功 – Sleep Practice. Also known as *shuixian gong* 睡仙功 (Sleeping Immortal Practice).

Sōng 鬆 – a state when tension is released; relaxed
• **fàngsōng** 放鬆 – to release tension

Qì 氣 – energy, life-force. Original literal meaning was the steam coming off a bowl of rice.
• **Qì** 炁 – precelestial original energy, the *qi* we refine in our body.
• **Qì** 炁 – the *qi* that we make in our body through neidan practice.

Qìgōng 氣功 – energy work or energy practice (note this is a modern term used to encapsulate a wide variety of Chinese practices, generally not a specific practice).

Qìchǎng 氣場 – energy field.

Qìxúe 氣穴 – Cavity of Qi; *xiatian* before there is anything within it. Actually, the *qixúe* is just an area of *qi* we use; it changes. It can be one of the Three Fields, or Three Spaces or even the whole inside of the body.

Qiángōng 乾宮 – Palace of Qian (heaven); another of the many terms for the *shangtian* (Upper Dantian).

Qìhùa 氣化 – *qi* transformation (it's a good thing, means stuff is going on during your session).

Qǐhuǒ 起火 – the Firing Process.
• **Jiuci qihuo** 九次起火 – the Nine Times Firing Process

Qiányīn 前陰 – (literally Front Yin) where the genitals attach to the torso, one of the three Lower Yin gates

Qīng lú 清爐 – Purifying the furnace (cleaning out energetic and emotional sludge from the body)

Qīqíng lìuyù 七情六慾) – seven emotions and six desires.

Quèqiáo 鵲橋 – Magpie Bridge. Spaces along the microcosmic orbit that need to be bridged.
- **Shàng quèqiáo** 上鵲橋 – Upper Magpie Bridge: mouth.
- **Xià quèqiáo** 下鵲橋 – Lower Magpie Bridge: anus.

Tàijí 太極 – literally "extreme poles". A state where there is difference and therefore perspective and relationship. Contrast *wuji*.

Tàijíquán 太極拳 – tai chi, an internal martial art.

Tiānmù 天目 – Celestial Eye (Third Eye). Used throughout the alchemical process to work with the Light of our Spirit.

Tiānmùxué 天目穴 – The Celestial Eye Point. Area between the eyebrows where the Celestial Eye looks outwards from the body. Also called the Upper Opening of the Mysterious Pass. This is an opening where *shen* can enter and exit the body, also where celestial and personal energies meet. *Ling* also gathers here. The scope of this area is larger than just the acupuncture point.

Tiānmén 天門 – energetic opening on the top of the head where *shen* can exit the body. In front of the *Baihui* but above the forehead, top of the Broken Line (vertical axis for the Three Fields). When closed, it is called the *dingmen*.

Tīng 聽 – hearing.
  i. **Yuan ting** 遠聽 – Far Hearing
  ii. **Jin ting** 近聽 – Near Hearing
  iii. **Fan ting** 反聽 – Return Hearing
  iv. **Nei ting** 內聽 – Inner Hearing

Wújí 無極 – literally "no poles". A state where there is no differentiation. Contrast *taiji*.

Wàidān 外丹 – external alchemy.

Wǔshù 五術 – The Five Arts. Often called the Five Taoist Arts. They include: fate calculation, appearance discernment, divination, practices, and medicine.

Wúwéi 無為 – allowing things and processes to happen on their own accord. The opposite of *youwei* 有為.

Wǔxíng 五行 – The Five Phases (also translated as "five elements" or "five agents") is a conceptual model used to understand our world.

Xiū Dào 修道 – Cultivate the Tao
- **xiūxíng dà dào** 修行大道 – cultivate the Tao
- **xiūliàn** 修煉 – practice; any practice that transforms the self
- **xiūliàn zhe** 修煉者 – practitioner
- **zìxiū** 自修 – self-cultivation

Xiāntiān 先天 – Precelestial, earlier heaven, before creation of phenomenal world; prenatal (Chinese med.). Opposite of *Houtian*.

Xiǎofù 小腹 – lower abdomen (below the belly button); inside this area is the Lower Space, *xiakong* 下空.

Xiǎoyào 小藥 – Lesser Medicine, Small Pill, Lesser Alchemical Ingredients. Also called Internal Medicine 內藥.

Xiàtían 下田 – the Lower Field, commonly referred to as the Lower Dantian. An important energy centre, a main focal point of practice.

Xìnggōng 性功 – Inner Nature Practice. Work that focuses on the more insubstantial and unchanging aspects of the self. Usually involves the Upper Field or Celestial Eye. Contrast with *Minggong*.
- **Xiuxing** 修性 – another term for cultivating our inner nature

Xíngjīn bǎgǔ 行筋拔骨 – practice that works the sinews and bones

Xíngyì quán 形意拳 – an internal martial art.

Xīnjìng 心靜 – stillness of mind. First major benchmark of Taoist cultivation.

Xiū bǔlòu 修無漏 – to energetically seal the body. Part of building foundation and preparation for *neidan*.

Xúanqiào 玄竅 – Mysterious opening. An energetic opening in the body. Where to? That's for us to find out.

Yěxìng 野性 – wild nature. Part of us controlled by our senses and desires.

Yìniàn 意念 – awareness and intention together.
- **Niàn** 念 – passive field of awareness; consciousness. *Yin*.
- **Yì** 意 – awareness with direction and movement; intention. *Yang*.
- **Lì** 力 (*Nianli* 念力) – power of our awareness. Also short for anchor point of awareness, *zhuoli dian* 著力點)

Yǐnxiān Methods 引仙法 – literally Attracting Immortality Methods. Dragon Gate preparatory methods used throughout Taoist alchemy.

Yìshi 意識 – passive field of awareness. It is used in conjunction with *yinian*, which is active. It is also used with our *shenyi*. *Yishi* is used after we have gone through the elixir training and are working on the sacred embryo and the Five Arts.

Yúnyǒu 雲遊 – Cloud Wandering.

Yǒuwei 有為 – the intentional doing of something to reach a goal. Opposite of *wuwei* 無為.

Zániàn 雜念 – random thoughts.

Zhànzhuāng 站樁 – standing post practice.

Zhēnrén 真人 – A practitioner who has completely reconciled their past, including their past lives.

Zhēnwǒ 真我 – the True Self.

Zhōngtían 中田 – the Middle Field, commonly referred to as the Middle Dantian. This energy centre is in the middle of the chest cavity on the level of the physical heart.

Zhōngxīn xiàn 中心線 – external centreline of body. Running from nose to navel on outside of body.

Zhōngzhèng xiàn 中正線 – internal centreline in body.

Zhōutīan gōng 周天功 – Micro, Macro, and Maoyou Cosmic Orbit practice.

Zhùjī 築基 – building foundation. Preparatory work for *neidan* practice.

Zhuóqì 濁氣 – turbid *qi*. It needs to be purified out of the body for success with *neidan* methods.

Zuòguān 坐關 – Barrier of Sitting. First major challenge of *neidan* practice.

Zhuǎnshì néngliàng 轉世能量 – reincarnation energy. Nasty karmic stuff that we want to clear out through our practice.

Essential Terms for Practice

The following Chinese terms are the basic vocabulary needed to follow the practices in this book.

Jīng 精: literally essence; energy associated with our physical body.

Nèidān 内丹: literally translates as internal cinnabar. Usually translated as internal alchemy. Note: there are several names for internal alchemy in Chinese.

Qì 氣: energy or life force
 Qì 炁: the *qi* we make in our body

Shén 神: literally spirit, the high-frequency energy of conscious awareness.

Shénguāng 神光: light of our spirit; spiritual illumination. The *shenguang* plays an important part in our practice and will be discussed more in later volumes. Because we use it during the opening of our *neidan* sessions in this volume, it is included as essential vocabulary.

Xiǎofù 小腹: the lower abdominal cavity, situated below the navel and housing the Lower Space 下空.

Xiàtián 下田: literally translates as Lower Field and commonly referred to as the Lower Dantian. An important energy centre, and a main focal point during the first phase of the alchemical work.

Yìnian 意念: a combination of awareness and intention.

Zhōngtián 中田: the Middle Field, commonly referred to as the Middle Dantian. This energy centre is in the middle of the chest cavity.

Made in the USA
Middletown, DE
06 May 2022

65366700R00121